MUNTJAC
Managing an Alien Species

Charles Smith-Jones

Illustrated by Ashley Boon

Published by Coch-Y-Bonddu Books
Machynlleth, Powys SY20 8DJ

www.anglebooks.com

ISBN 190478402X

Published 2004

Text © G.C.Smith-Jones

Design © Coch-Y-Bonddu Books, 2004

Chapter illustrations © Ashley Boon, 2004

All rights reserved. Without limiting the rights under copyright reserved above, no part of this publication may be reproduced, stored in or introduced into a retrieval system, or transmitted, in any form, or by any means (electronic, mechanical, photocopying, recording or otherwise) without the prior written permission of Coch-Y-Bonddu Books.

G.C.Smith-Jones has asserted his right under the Copyright, Designs and Patents Act, 1988, to be identified as Author of this work.

Designed and typeset in 11 on 13 point Bembo
by Jonathan Ward-Allen.

Printed and bound by The Cromwell Press, Trowbridge, Wiltshire

*For Sara, David and James,
and the families of stalkers everywhere*

Acknowledgements

Very rarely is a book a solo effort and this one is certainly no exception. I am indebted to many people who have shared their knowledge, provided photographs or offered advice, guidance and encouragement.

Foremost among them have been Norma Chapman, widely considered to be our leading authority on the muntjac in Britain, and Alex Jagger, whose name has been virtually synonymous with deer manager training for a long time now. Both have been my main critics in the preparation of the typescript and have been truly generous with their time, wisdom and honest advice.

I am also hugely grateful to His Grace the Duke of Bedford for his kind Foreword, and to the British Deer Society and the British Association for Shooting and Conservation for permission to include their Code of Practice for Deer Stalking as an appendix. There are many others who have also contributed. In no particular order, and with deep apologies to anyone that I may have inadvertently left out, they include:

A host of friends in the British Deer Society, particularly the Services Branch. Special mention must go to Rob Donaldson-Webster, Hugh Goodman, Dominic Griffith, John Hopkins, Nick Jasinski, Nick Lane, David Mullen, Hugh Rose, Jo Sharp and of course all at HQ BDS.

Ashley Boon, for his superb and evocative illustrations.

Bill Lash and Callum Thompson at Woburn.

David Field at Whipsnade.

Cyndy Brown and my own wife Sara for producing the recipes.

Gerald Collini, for a masterclass in muntjac calling.

Alan Haywood at Vicars Game, Reading.

Robinson's Butchers, Stockbridge.

And finally, I cannot finish without thanking Sara once again for her unstinting support and encouragement, Paul Morgan at Coch-y-Bonddu Books and Jon Ward-Allen at Medlar Press, without whom this book would never have made it into print.

Thanks go to the following for use of photographic material.
The Duke of Bedford and the Trustees of the Bedford Estates, The British Deer Society, Gerald Collini, Norman Dewhurst, Colin Dunton, Stephen Foster, Paul Gibbs, Dominic Griffith, Nick Lane, Adrian Mead, David Mullen, Ron Perkins, Hugh Rose.

Additional illustrations by the author.

Contents

Foreword 9

Introduction 11

Chapter 1   Introducing the Muntjac 15
        Origins & Fossil History
        Species & Natural Distribution
        Introduction to Britain
        Establishment & Spread
        Distribution Today
        Urban & Rural Populations
        Problem Areas
        Comparison with Other British Species

Chapter 2   Natural History of the Chinese Muntjac 29
        Size
        Pelage
        General Appearance & Movement
        Antlers – Size and Growth Cycle
        Teeth
        Social Structure and Territory
        Habitat and Foodstuffs
        Daily Life
        Breeding Cycle
        Communication
        Tracks, Trails & Signs
        Mortality

Chapter 3   Management Principles 55
        The Need to Cull
        Minimising Damage – Exclusion and Deterrents
        Public Considerations
        Urban Challenges
        Census Techniques, Acceptable Densities and a
           Balanced Population
        Cull Selection
        Basic Stalker Training
        Legal & Illegal Practices

Chapter 4	Equipment 75	

                    Calibres and Bullets
                      Rifles
                      Telescopic Sights
                      Sound Moderators
                      Other Rifle Fittings
                      Binoculars
                      Sticks
                      Clothing
                      Knives
                      Other Accessories

Chapter 5	Range Work 97	

                    Setting Up
                      Ammunition
                      Collimators & Bore Sighting
                      Basic Shooting Technique
                      Zeroing
                      The DSC1 Test (A Minimum Standard)
                      Advanced Practice
                      Rifle Maintenance

Chapter 6	Stalking Technique 113	

                    Camouflage & Concealment – Basic Principles
                      A Seasonal Approach
                      Locating & Spotting
                      Stalking
                      High Seats
                      Calling
                      Moving
                      The Shot
                      Reaction to Shot
                      The Follow-Up
                      Use of Dogs
                      Safety

Chapter 7	Carcase Handling & Preparation 145	

                    The Gralloch
                    Carcase Extraction and Storage

| | From Larder to Kitchen (Basic Butchery)
| | Trophy Preparation
| | Trophy Measurement
| | Taxidermy

Chapter 8   Health & Disease 169
            External Parasites – Ticks, Keds, Lice
            Internal Parasites
            Diseases
            The Lymph Nodes
            Suspect Health – Next Steps
            Oddities

Chapter 9   The Future 181
            Muntjac and Man
            Containment or Further Spread?
            Impact on Other Wildlife
            Commercial Potential
            The Venison Market
            Compulsory Deer Manager Training?
            A Need for Legislation?
            An Established Species

Appendix 1 Further Reading & Contacts 197
            Books
            Videos, DVDs and CD-Roms
            The Internet
            Deer Parks & Zoos
            Equipment
            Courses
            Trophy Measurement
            Societies and Organisations

Appendix 2 Muntjac Recipes 202

Appendix 3 Deer Stalking – A Code of Practice 206

Appendix 4 The British Deer Society 211

Index   213

I am delighted to have been asked to introduce this book on the muntjac; they are perhaps a much misunderstood species with an unfortunate reputation. I believe them to be delightful little deer, and I hope that this study will lead to a better appreciation of their value.

For the first half of the 20th century, muntjac were seen as an insignificant and largely benign presence in restricted parts of England. However they are now present in much of mainland Britain and still spreading; the situation has changed and unfortunately there are those who would seek their extermination.

Amongst others it was my ancestor, the 11th Duke of Bedford, who introduced muntjac to Britain in the 1890's. There are, of course, many muntjac enthusiasts out there who are happy to have these deer here, but if you are not a muntjac fan remember that without such enthusiasm the Père David deer would be but a distant memory.

This is a timely and welcome book. Charles Smith-Jones is clearly a muntjac aficionado, who recognizes the significant increase in numbers and distribution over recent decades and seeks to offer a practical way forward, which is both practical and humane. I strongly encourage people to manage the muntjac of Britain as we do here at Woburn; robustly, but with a deep affection and respect.

Bedford.

The Duke of Bedford   Woburn Abbey

INTRODUCTION

Over the past years I have become fascinated by the muntjac. On the estate in Hampshire where I manage the deer – predominantly roe – muntjac have increased from the occasional sighting to a substantial part in the annual cull, all in a few short years. This increase in numbers is reflected across the southern half of Britain. From modest beginnings in Bedfordshire, the muntjac now ranges to well above the Midlands, most of southern England and deep into Wales. And its distribution continues to expand.

Why is the muntjac so successful? How did an essentially tropical species establish itself in a country such as Britain, with an unwelcoming climate and high human population, all so different from its native home? There is no doubt that it has managed what must have seemed impossible when the first specimens were imported to this country just over a century ago.

The muntjac is truly an alien species, in looks and habits as well as origin. Of the six species of deer to be found in the wild in Britain it is the smallest in stature, and the only one without a fixed seasonal pattern for breeding. A muntjac buck is not the prettiest creature, yet it has a boxer dog type of appeal. Its hunched appearance and scurrying gait marks it out immediately as something different. I have alternately heard it described as a 'little hairy pig' by people trying to describe the unusual creature that crossed their path, or as a 'rat on stilts' by a journalist enraged by its depredations into his vegetable patch. One deer-loving estate manager, with whom I have an annual battle over my proposed roe cull, unashamedly swings the other way when it comes to muntjac and urges me to exterminate them all – I suspect that he would have no objections to machine guns or nerve gas if they were an option!

According to official figures, Britain today is host to an estimated wild muntjac population of some 100,000, expanding at a rate of at least 10% a year. In fact we have no real way of getting a proper idea of actual numbers and it is possible that this is an under-estimate. The muntjac probably outnumbers the native roe in some parts of England and, in some places, is claimed to be actively displacing them. Yet it is possible to live with muntjac practically on your doorstep and not even be aware of their presence – unless you are a keen gardener! That is because it is a creature of the undergrowth, preferring dense cover and rarely venturing out of it to feed. In some areas it is already a signif-

icant problem, causing damage to garden, field and plantation. In others it soon will be. Serious efforts are already being made to control the muntjac – with varying degrees of success and with equally varying degrees of humanity.

The muntjac is worth getting to know. He is so different from our other deer species that, as a relative newcomer, our knowledge of his way of life still remains incomplete. He can be a frustrating quarry – as any stalker whose sightings consist mainly of a small shape flitting across a track, or a raised white tail disappearing into the brambles, will testify! How unlike the roe, red, fallow and sika deer that are prepared to leave cover on a regular basis. Yet it is quite possible to get to grips with him. He certainly deserves better than to be treated as just another pest species, to be shot on sight without any thought or method. In fact, a little study and association with the muntjac quickly leads to a kind of addiction (as I know to my cost), such is the difference from 'normal' stalking.

Over the last twenty years or so a dedicated band of muntjac stalkers has grown up, originally in the Midlands but spreading, like the deer itself, across the rest of the country. There is a great deal of muntjac knowledge out there but to date a lot of it has not been set down on paper. That is perhaps the main purpose, and I hope the value, of this book. Over the last twenty years or so any number of excellent publications have become available to the stalker, but the muntjac tends only to get a brief mention and has never seemed to merit its own volume. For stalkers, muntjac are an unusual and demanding quarry which require a different approach if they are to be successfully managed, so I hope here to be able to put matters right.

There is another reason. I clearly remember back in the mists of time when I shot my first roe. In the absence of a mentor, everything – the stalk, the shot, the gralloch, skinning and jointing – was done from what I had available to me in book form (I think that it was Richard Prior's excellent little booklet published jointly by the Game Conservancy and the British Deer Society). I would have been lost without it. Although there is no beating the presence of an experienced stalker to guide and teach the novice, or attending one of the recognised courses available to the budding stalker, I hope that this handbook will be the next best thing. It's always good to have something to refer to when you need it.

Finally, I hope to be able to shed some light on the habits of the muntjac and perhaps upgrade his value as a fascinating, if often unwelcome, addition to our British fauna. Decried by many as a pest, he deserves better treatment than he gets at the hands of some. In the pages to come I hope to be able to increase understanding of this supremely adaptable and elusive animal and point to a way forward in the management of an alien, but firmly established, species.

Chapter 1
Introducing the Muntjac

Origins & Fossil History
The muntjac is a survivor. It has walked the Earth with long-gone creatures such as mastodons, ground sloths and giant beavers, and been preyed upon by the likes of sabre-tooth cats and bear dogs, as well as by early man and his ancestors. It has seen other species of large mammal evolve, multiply and then die out, and has existed on our planet through ice ages and climate upheaval. It still, remarkably, thrives in the same form today as it did in the Miocene epoch.
It has been described as a walking fossil. It is certainly one of the most ancient species of deer in the world today. It was present in Europe at least 15 million years ago and its bones have been discovered in deposits in France and Germany dating back to the Miocene. Since the early Pleistocene, however – perhaps 2 million years ago – its fossils have only been found in Eastern Asia.

The muntjac and its only other living relative, the Tufted deer of southern China and northern Burma, evolved from *Dicrocerus*, a small deer from the

The muntjac has changed little since the Miocene epoch

Middle Miocene period which had antlers with two tines on each side, long pedicles and small tusks. Both the muntjac and the Tufted deer share these features. *Dicrocerus* is an important fossil deer because it is the first clear evidence of a deer which shed and regrew its antlers annually (known as a deciduous species) as opposed to having horns as a permanent growth. Within the family *Cervidae*, which covers all of the deer species, muntjac have their own sub family *Muntiacinae*.

There are few more primitive modern deer than the muntjac. One species is the Chinese Water deer, which is characterised by a complete lack of antlers and more highly developed canine tusks. To bring the muntjac's antiquity as a species into perspective, the earliest evidence of Roe deer only goes back one million years or so, and the Fallow deer in its modern form only began to appear as recently as 100,000 years ago. The Giant Deer Megaloceros only appeared 11,000 years ago, and was extinct by 500 BC at the latest. Its demise has been alternately put down to climate change, over-specialisation or disease.

Species and Natural Distribution
There are several distinct species of muntjac, the natural distribution for all of these being various parts of Asia. The Indian muntjak, *Muntiacus muntjak*, is the most widespread. It has 15 subspecies which are to be found across India and as far as Vietnam on the mainland, as well as on the islands of Sri Lanka, Sumatra, Borneo and Java. *Muntjak* is, in fact, the native name for these deer in the Sunda language of western Java and it is for this reason that this species is specifically spelt with a 'k'. All of the subspecies are very similar in colour – a deep chestnut which is slightly darker on the animals back. A distinct winter coat is slightly darker. A buck will stand about 23 inches high at the shoulder and weigh some 40 lb; the antlers can reach over 5 inches long in some of the subspecies, one of which (found in Myanmar, formerly Burma) can produce antlers almost 7 inches long

The Chinese or Reeves muntjac, *M. reevesi*, has two subspecies, one in eastern China and the other on the island of Taiwan. Its alternative name is derived from one John Reeves, an Assistant Inspector of Tea with the East India Company in the early 1800s, who is credited with bringing the first specimen to Britain (it is also after him that the Reeves pheasant is named). Very similar to the Indian muntjac in colour, the Chinese species is only a slightly richer shade of chestnut, but is almost 3 inches smaller at the shoulder. Its antlers tend not to grow as long. The Chinese muntjac is considered to be the most primitive of all the muntjac species and is the one of most interest to us from a British perspective.

Fea's muntjac, *M. feae*, is found in Thailand. It is dark brown in colour with yellow hairs around the crown of the pedicles and at the base of the ears.

Roosevelt's muntjac, *M.rooseveltorum*, is found in Vietnam and is similar to the Chinese muntjac but slightly more red in colour, and the Black muntjac, *M.crinifrons*, is confined to eastern China. As its name suggests, it is a blackish-brown in colour. The Yellow muntjac, *M.atherodes*, specific to Borneo, was granted status as a separate species in 1982 after a long period of being considered an Indian muntjak subspecies. It is a yellowish orange with a distinctive dark dorsal stripe.

Since the 1980s, helped perhaps by the relaxation of political boundaries, more new species of muntjac have come to light. The remote Truong Son range of mountains in Vietnam have yielded two that were previously unknown to science, and for all we know there may be more. The Giant muntjac, *Megamuntiacus vuquangensis*, was first recorded in 1994 in the Vu Quang Nature reserve in Vietnam. Its range seems to extend as far as Laos and Cambodia. It is truly a giant among muntjacs, being twice as big as any previously-known species and with adult males weighing up to 110 lbs. The Truong Son muntjac, *M.truongsonensis*, was discovered in the same area at around the same time, weighing in a more average 33lbs or so; it was only confirmed as a new species in 1997. In the same year, Myanmar produced the diminutive Leaf muntjac, *M.putaoensis*, which weighs some 25 lbs – its name comes from the local hunters habit of transporting it wrapped in a leaf.

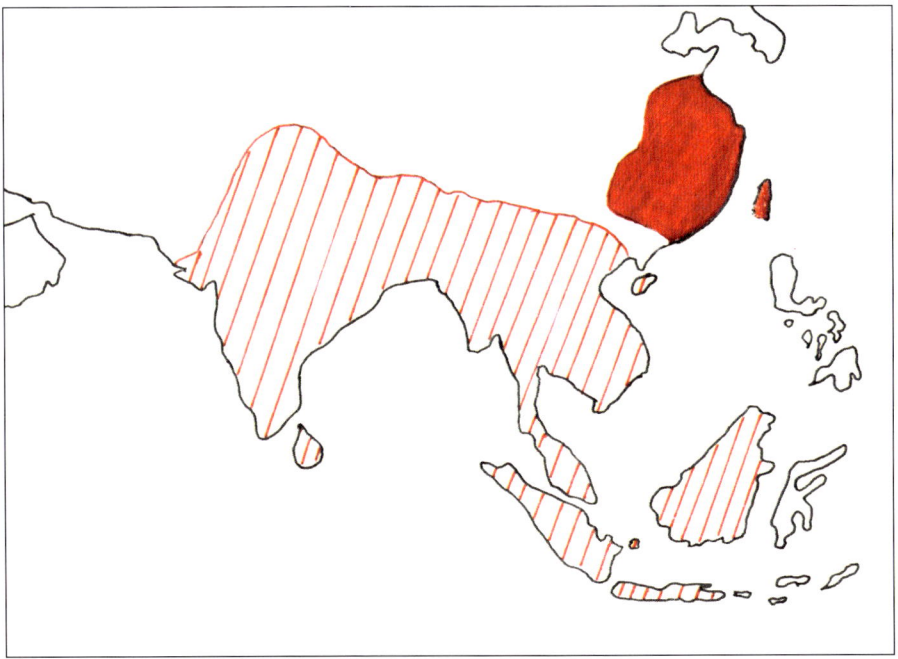

The Asian range of muntjac deer. The distribution of the Chinese muntjac (including that of the Taiwanese subspecies) is shown in solid red.

It would be unreasonable to rule out the possibility that there are more 'undiscovered' muntjac species out there, doubtless well-known to local people but still waiting to be described scientifically.

Behavioural patterns seem to be broadly similar across the species, and these will be covered in the next chapter. Two features of this deer are worth noting, though. One is its habit of barking for periods of up to an hour when disturbed or excited, and another is the unique feature of pedicles which extend down the front of the bucks forehead. These give rise to its alternative English names of 'Barking Deer' and 'Rib Faced Deer'.

Introduction to Britain

It is generally accepted that muntjac were first introduced into Britain by the 11th Duke of Bedford, an avid collector of deer species, who maintained the deer park at Woburn in Bedfordshire. The original introduction was of Indian muntjak in 1893. These were liberated in the woods both inside and outside the park and quickly established themselves. It quickly proved an unsatisfactory choice however, as this species is particularly noted for is aggression. The story goes that, after a very brief period at large and the killing of a favourite dog by one of these deer, the Duke ordered that the entire population should be shot out. Whatever the truth, attempts were made to eradicate the Indian muntjak which were replaced by the smaller Chinese variety, the first of which arrived in 1894.

Woburn Abbey, main site of the first British muntjac introductions

Some time around the early 1890s attempts were also made to introduce muntjac to France but there is no evidence that they ever became established in the wild there. They do exist in a number of French estates and collections, but Britain is the only country outside the muntjac's natural Asiatic range with a truly wild and thriving population.

Woburn has not, of course, been the only point of entry for muntjac into this country. There have been any number of private collections which chose to keep them. Whipsnade Zoo, a close neighbour of Woburn, certainly provided escapees. Being a small and largely solitary deer, they are better suited to enclosures than the larger, herding species. They are also better escapologists – a muntjac can fit through the smallest of gaps – and it was inevitable that animals escaped their enclosures and established themselves in the wild at many points other than Woburn.

Both World Wars helped to augment wild populations when, with estate workers called up to serve in the Forces, fences and other containing boundaries were allowed to fall into disrepair. Woburn itself was requisitioned for Army use during the Second World War and the failure of soldiers to keep the gates closed allowed a further escape of muntjac (as well as other deer species) to boost the wild population.

It is highly unlikely that attempts to eradicate the Indian muntjak population at Woburn were entirely

The 11th Duke of Bedford, credited with introducing the first muntjac at Woburn

Muntjac are a popular deer species in zoos and private collections

Muntjac roam freely about Whipsnade Zoo and co-exist peacefully with some unusual bedfellows; these are mara, a South American rodent.

successful and even until recently there have been claims that Britain still supports a number. There have also been suggestions that a degree of hybridisation occurred between Indian and Chinese animals. This is entirely possible, as it has happened under zoo conditions although the progeny have always been sterile. Under wild conditions, however, hybridisation is comparatively rare and it has never been proven in the British population. Given a choice between one of its kind and a close relative, a species will normally opt for its own in any case.

Although rumours persist of the presence of Indian muntjak, British animals have all the characteristics of the Chinese variety as well as a matching chromosome count. It is now fairly safe to assume that this is the only muntjac species that we have established in our country. For the remainder of this book all reference to muntjac will assume the Chinese variety unless specified otherwise.

Establishment and Spread
By the 1950s, only half a century after its introduction to Britain, the muntjac was firmly established in our country. However the population remained largely centred on Bedfordshire and Hertfordshire. Two major factors had assisted its success. Firstly, its arrival coincided with the decay of some of the large estates after two World Wars and a shift in approaches to land management. Secondly, the Forestry Commission was embarking in a replanting programme. The results of both was a profusion of habitat perfectly suited to the needs of this secretive and unobtrusive little deer.

Nor was it seen as any kind of a threat to the environment. Existing in relatively small numbers and rarely observed, it was perceived as a curiosity that caused little damage. General feeling was that, as a jungle species, it would be more susceptible to the British weather which would prevent any significant population growth. Certainly during the severe winter conditions in 1962 – 63 there were massive numbers of deaths (over 70 bodies were found in one forest alone) but muntjac have proved to be remarkably resilient, with fawns born during mid-winter having excellent chances of survival under more usual circumstances. Over the past few decades, a tendency towards mild winters has assisted them further.

Lacking any significant trophy value, muntjac were not considered a game species and paid any particular attention. In its native Asia, the muntjac is a prey species with no shortage of natural predators. In Britain, foxes will account for a number of fawns. Otherwise, apart from motor vehicles and dogs (and of course, rumoured big cats), there are no predators. The other deer species, also lacking natural predators but controlled by man, were kept in check and tended to avoid his close proximity. Muntjac have not proved to be so fussy in this respect. As long as a suitable habitat existed, they would use it and a suitably overgrown suburban garden fitted the bill quite nicely. In effect, an empty niche had been discovered and filled.

By the early 1980s it was clear that numbers were really on the increase. The species was resident in a large area of land covering central southern England and the Midlands, and there had been sightings as far afield as Cumbria, Yorkshire, Denbighshire, Gloucestershire and Cornwall. Even if some of these were of animals that had escaped from zoos or private collections – which continued to happen – there was no doubt that the population was spreading rapidly. At the time it was estimated that the rate was one mile a year.

Distribution Today

A glance at the distribution map shows that, if you live anywhere in England and Wales, you are probably not too far from muntjac country.

Able to live in close proximity to man without being readily observed, the muntjac has only recently come to be seen as a potential problem

The species is certainly now widespread and still extending its range. The population remains centred on the Midlands but now extends to the southern counties of England, across to Norfolk and well over the Welsh borders. Wales itself is seeing previously isolated populations, probably originating from escapes or deliberate introductions, beginning to grow and spread, and doubtless these too will eventually join with the main body. The only real barrier to movement seems to be large tracts of inhospitable country which the muntjac are reluctant to cross – wide open spaces with little cover are boundaries which help to contain the deer. Populations of other deer species already established in an area do not seem to offer any real disincentive to colonisation. If the muntjac find a habitat that agrees with them they are likely to stay.

At the time of writing there is no sign of a significant muntjac population in Scotland, although there have been isolated sightings and it is very likely that there are already viable populations in some Border areas, as well as even further north, if anecdotal evidence is to be believed. The Deer Commission for Scotland is currently seeking to gather hard proof of just how many muntjac there actually are, and where the populations are centred. That is not to say that Scotland is likely to be exempt from a wider population as their range grows and muntjac continue to adapt to our climate – especially if we are experiencing the global warming that many claim with increasing credibility.

Isolated sightings continue to come in from some very unlikely places – some as far north as Inverness, or on the island of Skomer off the Welsh coast. Once again, assuming correct identification, escapees or deliberate introductions are the most likely cause. Muntjac remain popular as a decorative small deer for zoos and collections, and escapes will doubtless continue to reinforce wild populations.

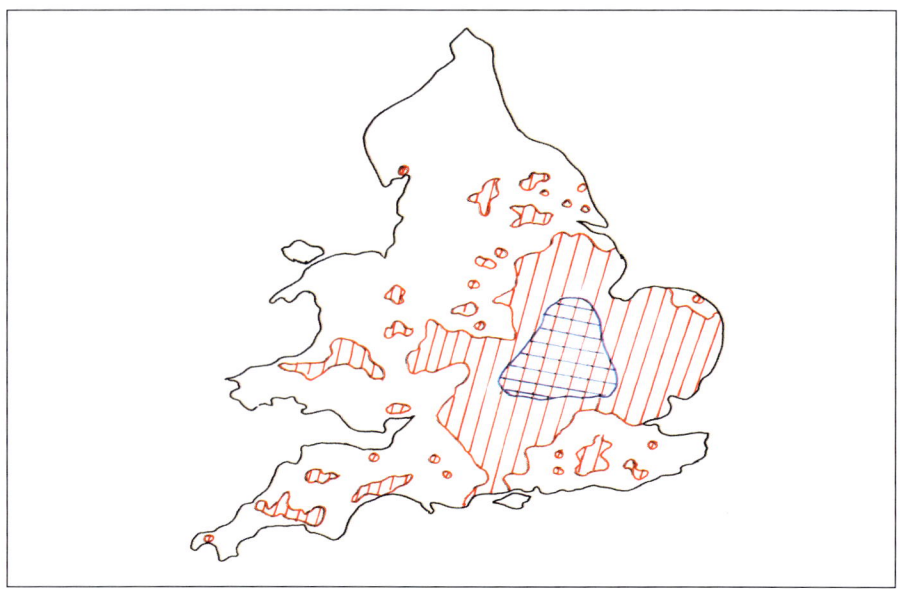

The distribution of muntjac in England and Wales today is shown in red, while the blue area represents the situation in 1965. The pockets of populations outside the core area are a clear indication of either deliberate introductions or escapees from collections establishing themselves in the wild.

Urban and Rural Populations

The muntjac is without doubt one of our most cosmopolitan deer. It will tuck itself away into most kinds of habitat, provided that it can find the seclusion that it needs to feel secure. Close proximity to man does not seem to worry it unduly. Gardens are visited regularly, and not exclusively under cover of darkness. In fact, the muntjac will become remarkably tolerant of human presence as long as it does not feel threatened. The first sign of a local population is very often a nocturnal garden raider that becomes sufficiently confident to return during the hours of daylight.

Once they feel secure, muntjac can become very bold in the presence of man even during daylight hours

Railway embankments, used and unused, are also popular. They provide dense bramble thickets which provide food, cover and shelter. The thunder of locomotives passing by regularly is not a problem and muntjac can be frequently spotted, feeding totally unconcerned, by commuters approaching a main line station. Muntjac are no different from other deer; as a prey species, their flight mechanism is very keenly developed and they quickly learn to differentiate between what is a threat and what is safe. To constantly run from everything wastes energy – hence they are able to decide what to tolerate and what not to.

The countryside offers different, but equally acceptable, opportunities. It is not an accident that areas managed for game shooting are popular with this little deer. A thick, warm woodland understorey holds muntjac just as well as game birds, providing food and safety. Nor, it seems, do the deer seem confined to the more densely wooded areas. They can establish themselves in the most unlikely of places and a small population was first confirmed on the grassland of Salisbury Plain in Wiltshire during the 1990s, moving freely between small plantations and gorse patches.

It is this adaptability which has helped the muntjac's spread within Britain, and which will doubtless allow it to expand to any part of the country that can support it. It is very likely that, in Britain, the only parts unlikely to meet their needs are the less hospitable and more exposed areas of uplands. Otherwise, wherever there is suitable forage and shelter from the elements there are eventually likely to be muntjac.

Any woodland with the cover to support game birds will attract muntjac

Problem Areas

As numbers grew, it became apparent that muntjac were not the benign presence that they were first thought to be. Their small size enables them to get into enclosures that keep out the larger deer and, to add insult to injury, they are better jumpers than their stocky build suggests. Fencing is no deterrent. If they cannot go through it (and it is surprising how easily this is done – if the head fits, the body can often follow) they will go under or over if it is not high enough or securely dug in.

Gardeners were the first to notice levels of damage, mistakenly thinking that roe deer were responsible. Raiders (not necessarily nocturnal, and increasingly in daylight as animals become bolder) find

Muntjac are adept at breaching inadequate fencing. This chicken wire has simply been pushed through.

rich pickings in flower beds, borders and vegetable patches. Intrusions into gardens can be infuriating – muntjac are no diplomats, and always quick to try something different. They are no respecters of the exotic and the expensive!

Although there is any number of market gardeners who will argue the point, agricultural damage is not a huge problem although it cannot be totally discounted. New growth is always attractive to deer, but as a crop establishes itself they will start to forage elsewhere unless the population is at an especially high density. Muntjac will often decamp into standing crops in the summer months, and their presence there may lead to the assumption that they are feeding on them. This is not necessarily true. Very frequently deer seen feeding in crops are actually selecting out other plants that grow among them. And inevitably where large scale damage has occurred, if a deer is seen at the scene of the crime it is automatically condemned as responsible – no matter if rabbits or hares may be the true villains!

Unprotected new growth or plantings can be quickly targeted by a foraging deer

Forestry is at its most vulnerable when newly planted. Although muntjac will browse new tree growth and strip bark, sensible levels of protection will allow young trees to grow unmolested to a point where they are of less interest to the deer. Compared to the damage that other species of deer can do to larger trees by fraying, bole scoring or large scale bark stripping, the muntjac is a minor offender. Of far greater worry is the impact that a growing muntjac population can have on their environment and the other wildlife that it supports. As ground level browsers, too many muntjac can thin out a woodland understorey to the extent that ground nesting birds, small mammals and invertebrates and others find their habitat disappearing. Competition for forage can especially affect roe deer. High numbers of muntjac have been proven to cause considerable degradation of bluebells and other specific ground flora, especially where they are in relatively isolated areas of preferred habitat or where they have been enclosed (either accidentally or for deliberate research).

Bluebells are one of the plant species under threat from large numbers of muntjac

Woodland in spring; muntjac will actively seek out new growth.

Road traffic accidents are a growing problem area, particularly in areas of high muntjac and high motor vehicle densities. We have already seen that they are happy to coexist alongside man, and roadside verges are often a source of attractive forage. All deer are no respecters of the Highway Code and many are killed on our roads every year. Although muntjac may seem insignificant in size compared with, say, a big fallow buck, the effect of hitting 40lbs or so of solid object in a car travelling at speed cannot be discounted, and the result of a collision could be as costly to the driver as it is to the deer.

Comparison with Other British Species

There are six species of deer commonly resident in Britain, of which the muntjac is one. Fallow were most probably first brought to these shores by the Normans (some claim even earlier by the Romans), and sika and Chinese Water deer were introduced at around the same time as the muntjac from the same parts of the world. Of the Asian species, the success of the muntjac has been by far the most spectacular although the sika has done very well wherever conditions have suited it.

Only two of our deer species, the red and the roe, are native to this country. Even the roe, often thought of as the most British of deer, cannot be considered to be truly native in its current form. Originally common across the British Isles but persecuted to virtual extinction, the thriving roe population in England today is largely the result of reintroductions (often with Continental stock) during the 18th and 19th Centuries. Only the Scottish roe can be considered to come from a truly native strain.

We can easily discount the possibility of confusing muntjac with red, sika and fallow deer simply on the basis of size alone. These are all large deer which dwarf the diminutive muntjac. There is a common confusion among non-experts with roe and Chinese Water deer, which are closer to the muntjac in size (if not in appearance) although the former are more classically deer-shaped to look at, with longer legs and necks in proportion to their bodies. The roe is somewhat larger than the muntjac but has no visible tail. The Chinese Water deer is slightly closer in size but it is more lightly built and, unlike the muntjac, the tail is not so obvious and males do not carry antlers.

Comparative sizes of British deer (left to right): 6' man, fallow, roe, muntjac, Chinese Water deer, sika and red

A fleeting glimpse of a muntjac might cause the casual observer to think that it is a fox, especially if it is moving in cover. It may seem difficult to confuse the two species, but they are both of a similar size and it is a common mistake. In fact, once you know what you are looking at it is difficult to confuse the muntjac with any creature living wild in this country. It is marked out by its small size, short legs in proportion to the body and generally pig-like appearance.

Wild boar seem to be establishing themselves in parts of southern Britain, specifically Sussex and Devon at the time of writing, themselves escapees from captivity just as muntjac were initially. Although the muntjac is pig-like in appearance, there is little likelihood that the two could be mistaken. The wild boar is obviously heavily built, has the distinct snout, and a longer-haired, darker coat. The muntjac is smooth-coated, longer-legged and positively dainty in comparison. Even to an inexperienced observer, the fleeing muntjac's flag of a tail is the certain giveaway.

Roe buck – long legs & neck, sophisticated antlers on short pedicles, no visible tail

Chinese Water deer buck – long legs & neck, no antlers, visible canines, short tail

Muntjac buck – short legs & neck, rudimentary antlers on long hairy pedicles, hunched pig-like appearance, visible tail

CHAPTER 2
Natural History of the Chinese Muntjac

Size

With a typical mature buck standing some 50cm (19 inches) at the shoulder, the muntjac is physically the smallest of our native deer, about the size of a springer spaniel. The next up in size, Chinese Water deer, are only slightly taller but are not so heavily built and lack the compact, muscular appearance of the muntjac. Does tend to be slightly smaller on average, but only by a couple of centimetres.

There appears to be a considerable degree of variation in body weights, even within the same parts of the country. An average 2-year old buck will weigh in at around 14 kg (31 lbs), whilst a doe would be just less at around 12 kg (27 lbs). It is especially difficult to be specific about female weights, however, as

A mature muntjac is little larger than a springer spaniel

mature does are inevitably at some stage of pregnancy. The weights given are for a live animal; stalkers more often refer to the weight of carcases dressed for the larder (i.e. with head, forelegs and internal organs removed). Dressed weight is about 65% of live weight as a very general guideline.

Muntjac do, of course, get much bigger than this. Mature animals of 17 kg (38 lbs) are common, and weights up to 20 kg (44 lbs) are regularly recorded. I am aware of one Norfolk specimen that went into the larder at 15 kg (33 lbs), indicating a live weight of around 23 kg (50 lbs).

The muntjac fawn weighs in at around 1 kg (just over 2 lbs) at birth and gains weight rapidly. Until it is weaned at around six or seven weeks old, it is estimated that weight gain can be as high as 1 kg per fortnight. By the time that it is about seven months old it will weigh around 10 kg (22 lbs).

Pelage
The summer coat of the muntjac is a rich, glossy chestnut-brown, while the underparts (the belly and inside of the haunches) can range from off-white or buff to a pale grey. The outer surfaces of the forelegs are a darker brown, and there can be hints of a pale patch on the throats of both bucks and does.

A muntjac buck in summer coat, showing the pale underparts

The winter coat begins to grow through from September onwards, and is usually complete by the beginning of November. It is a darker grey/brown in colour, retaining the paler underparts. The forelegs of bucks turn almost black at this time of year.

The winter coat is darker, and adds an impression of bulk to the animal

Whilst the change into winter coat is a gradual affair, that to the summer coat is far more obvious. It starts in April and may not be complete until June - for much of this period the animal looks very scruffy and unkempt.

The tail can measure up to 17 cm (6^1/$_2$ inches) long. Throughout the year its underside is white, as is the area around the vent, and the top retains a slightly more ginger tinge than the rest of the coat. The white edging to the tail is just visible when viewing an undisturbed animal - it becomes doubly so when the animal, if alarmed, raises its tail in the characteristic muntjac alarm posture.

The white underside of the tail is clearly visible in this photograph

A fleeing animal with its tail raised – a clear signal to any others in the vicinity

Facial markings vary between the sexes. Bucks have a black line which extends the length of the pedicles, creating a characteristic 'V' when the animal is viewed head-on. In comparison, does have a kite shaped patch on the forehead which ranges from dark brown to almost black. The heads of both sexes contain two sets of glands, both of which are obvious in the living animal. The frontal glands are easily visible as two parallel lines measuring about 4 cm ($1\frac{1}{2}$ inches) on the forehead, and the even larger sub-orbital glands are situated in large sockets in front of each eye.

Muntjac does have a kite shaped patch on the forehead.
The dorsal stripe along the back, which both sexes have, is also especially obvious in this photograph.

The V shape of the black lines running up each pedicle is typical of a muntjac buck.

Fawns are born a mid-brown in colour, with a darker chestnut stripe down the back. The crown of the head is dark, and the fluffy hair on the lower jaw gives a bearded appearance. The sub-orbital gland is obvious from birth. They are covered in off-white spots which are arranged in horizontal lines along each side. These spots start to disappear when the fawn reaches six weeks old, and have usually completely faded three to four weeks later.

A muntjac fawn; the tail, dark crown of the head and obvious sub-orbital gland distinguish it from the young of other deer

Although albinism and melanism have been recorded in muntjac, such instances are rare compared to other deer. In addition to some variety in the shade of the underparts, a population may contain some animals which are only slightly lighter or darker than others. Generally speaking, though, muntjac tend to be uniform in colour and (so far) there is no real sign of any variation between regional populations in the UK.

General Appearance and Movement

The general appearance of the muntjac is porcine, or pig-like. For a deer its legs are relatively short, and its body is thick-set. Characteristically the rump remains higher than the shoulder when standing or running, and the animal will frequently stand with an arched back. The head is usually held low in relation to the raised rump even when moving at speed, although a static alert animal will crane its head if it needs to increase visibility. Unless alarmed, the tail is held close to the body.

The muntjac is pig-like in appearance

Normal movement is a pottering gait - muntjac seldom stand still for long, and frequently feed 'on the hoof', taking food items as they pass along a trail. They have a swinging trot reminiscent of that of a small pony. If disturbed they run surprisingly quickly and are not impeded by the thickest of cover. Such sprinting is fluid and does not incorporate any form of bounding, but cannot be maintained over long distances. Like most young deer, muntjac fawns will indulge in play, dashing about at high speed and kicking their hind legs out. Sometimes small pieces of wood are thrown about as part of the game.

Antlers - Size and Growth Cycle
Compared to most species of deer, the muntjac buck carries only the most rudimentary of antlers. A representative mature animal would be likely to carry two single spikes, each ending in a backward and inward-pointing curve, with perhaps a small brow tine facing forward at the base. Anything more is unusual. The outside length of an antler is typically about 8 - 10 cm (3 - 4 inches); certainly anything over 14 cm (5½ inches) is exceptional.

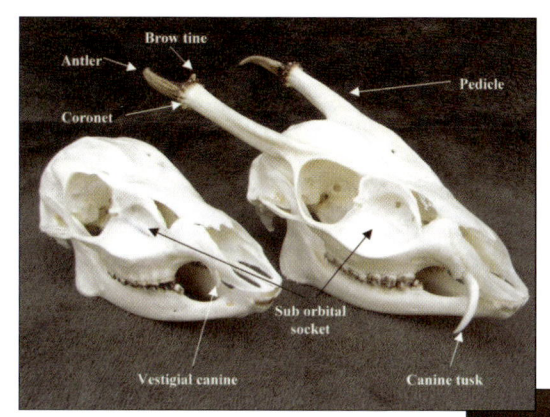

Skulls of muntjac buck (right) and doe showing the principal aspects

(L to R) First head – antlers no more than an extension of the pedicles. Mature – obvious coronets and brow points have developed, pedicles shortening with successive antler casting and regrowth. Old – short pedicles, heavy antlers.

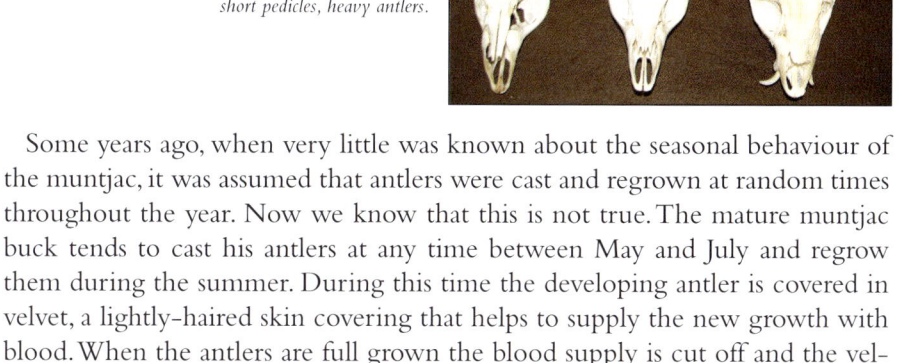

Some years ago, when very little was known about the seasonal behaviour of the muntjac, it was assumed that antlers were cast and regrown at random times throughout the year. Now we know that this is not true. The mature muntjac buck tends to cast his antlers at any time between May and July and regrow them during the summer. During this time the developing antler is covered in velvet, a lightly-haired skin covering that helps to supply the new growth with blood. When the antlers are full grown the blood supply is cut off and the velvet dies, to be rubbed off on suitable vegetation – young saplings are especially popular for this activity. Antlers are usually hard and clean by September at the latest.

However, as muntjac can breed at any time of the year, it is not so simple with a young buck's first head. This has to be grown and then fall in line with the adult cycle for casting and regrowth. The pedicles from which the antlers grow do not start to develop on the immature buck until he is about five months old; the first set of antlers develops on these from any time after eight months. These first antlers are normally little more than short spikes or knobs with no coronet or brow tine, measuring no more than 2 - 3 cm ($^3/_4$ - 1 inch). They are retained until the animal is able to fall in with the adult cycle - therefore, if a buck is born in December of Year One, it will grow its first antlers in August of Year Two but keeps them until May of Year Three. It is, of course, possible for a buck to complete its first antler cycle within a year - but only if it is born at the right time.

A few individual animals seem to contradict this cycle, and mature muntjac bucks in hard horn consistently turn up during the summer months when the

A mature buck in velvet

A mature buck pictured in mid-August, in the process of cleaning the velvet from his newly-grown antlers

A buck's first antler is little more than an extension of the pedicle

Portrait of a representative mature buck

vast majority are in velvet. Just why this is so, and why there is such a wide variation in the times that casting normally takes place, remains a mystery. It is quite possible that, given the muntjac's status as a very primitive form of deer, the hormonal influences that govern casting and regrowth are simply weaker than those that affect the more modern deer species. It is even possible that some bucks might even carry their antlers for more than a year before renewing them; certainly we still have much to learn about this aspect of the muntjac's natural history.

Studies of specific muntjac populations in Asia (where the seasons are less marked by extremes of climate) have shown a less distinct tendency towards seasonality in antler cycles but no truly hard and fast rules for all animals. In these studies all bucks observed between November and February were in hard antler, but about a fifth of them were also in the same condition during July. Here, at least, there is some commonality with the British situation, as I have never heard of a mature buck being seen in velvet during the winter months.

Teeth

Both male and female muntjac have canine tusks. The female canine is vestigial, and does not protrude more than 5mm (1/4 inch) outside the gum. The male canine is much more apparent, growing downwards, backwards and outwards to a length of 4cm (1 1/2 inches). When fully developed they are visible just protruding from the side of the mouth of the living animal. The rear edge is extremely sharp, as is the tip (something to bear in mind when handling a dead animal, or dealing with an injured one). Bucks use them for fighting and fraying – as a result it is common to find mature bucks with one or both canines broken. Fraying serves not only to mark territory, but helps to keep the edge of the tusk sharp. The tusks can be moved in their sockets a few millimetres, but are otherwise not particularly mobile.

As a buck gets older, the opening at the top of the canine tusk gradually closes over

The young of both sexes produce a non-permanent upper canine tusk, and in the case of bucks the permanent tusk starts to grow alongside it once the animal is about five months old - sometimes the two can be found together but the 'baby' tusk is soon shed. The permanent tooth grows very quickly, and by the time the animal is a year old it will have reached 2 cm ($^3/_4$ inch); thereafter growth slows down. The female canine growth cycle is different, the permanent tooth not erupting until the animal is around a year old and of course not growing to much larger than the deciduous tooth.

Of the other teeth, the third premolar on the lower jaw has three ridges or 'cusps' in the immature animal; about eighteen months old the permanent tooth erupts from below it and has only two cusps. This tooth growth cycle is a useful way of determining - or at least estimating - the age of a dead animal. Once the deer has it's adult teeth, age estimation can be based on degrees of tooth wear (a deer's teeth do not regenerate as they wear down over the years). Tooth wear will vary greatly from place to place, and depends heavily on the variety of roughage eaten as well as the general grittiness of the soil types. Muntjac teeth do not seem to wear as rapidly as those of other deer.

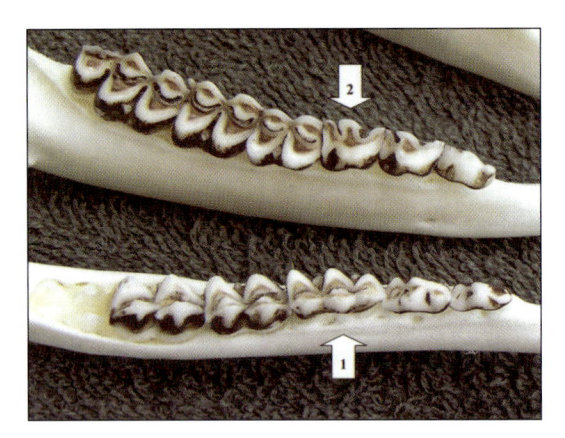

Comparison of the teeth of a mature muntjac (top) and the incomplete dentition of a juvenile. Until the animal is about 12 months old, its third premolar has three cusps (Arrow 1). After this point the permanent adult tooth with two cusps (Arrow 2) erupts from behind it.

Here, the adult third premolar can be seen erupting from below the juvenile tooth

Social Structure and Territory

It has long been assumed that muntjac were a solitary and unsociable species; as they have spread, however, so has our understanding of them. While we still have a lot to learn, much more is now known about their social structure. Whilst not a herding species, such as red, fallow or sika, they are not as solitary as roe - which can be particularly intolerant of each other, especially during the spring and summer months.

Muntjac fall somewhere in the middle. While they do not form true herds, numbers of animals are quite content to exist side by side and share communal feeding areas (a sort of 'no-mans land'), even if there is little interaction between them. In zoo and park collections large numbers of muntjac are often kept together, but it is noticeable that these enclosed 'herds' are predominantly female. It is fair to say that antagonism only comes into play where territory and breeding are involved. Generally speaking, however, unless you live in an area where the muntjac population is particularly high, most of your sightings are likely to be of lone animals.

Aggression is more likely to occur between bucks when a doe is in oestrus in the immediate locality. Here a small doe, probably coming into season for the first time, receives the attentions of a buck while a mature doe (very likely her mother) looks on

It is now widely accepted that bucks do maintain territories - the more capable the buck, the larger the territory. Does also maintain home ranges, but these are not strictly territories as they can overlap with those of other does, and studies have indicated that their average size is about twelve hectares. The buck's territory may be as much as twice the size of the doe's home range, but only seldom overlap with the territory of another buck. It is quite likely, though to overlap with a number of doe's home ranges. As there is no bonding between buck and doe, he will mate with as many of these does as he can. By the same token, a doe in oestrus will probably mate with any number of bucks whose territories her range overlaps.

Territories and home ranges can be relatively small, the main criteria being that they include suitable cover and forage throughout the year. Female offspring are likely to set up their own home ranges in the same area as their mother so, where an area is not overpopulated, does seen together are quite likely to be related. Sightings of bucks, does and immature animals may not, as previously supposed, be family parties - bucks are tolerant of other animals unless another buck is a direct challenge to their territory, and thus their breeding rights.

Bucks will physically fight over territories, but before this happens other forms of aggressive behaviour are likely to take place first. Rivals will scrape the ground with a forefoot, click their teeth and engage in parallel walking as they size up each other's relative strength. If one will not back down at this stage, physical engagement will take place after a series of false advances and retreats. The bucks will engage in a shoving match using antlers, pedicles and foreheads, each pushing and twisting in an attempt to throw their opponent off balance. The buck that succeeds in doing this will then attempt to slash his adversary with his tusks, aiming for face, ears or neck (the skin of the neck is especially thick as a protection against this) - or rump, in the case of a fleeing opponent. Tusks get broken during this process - the buck with a broken tusk is at a serious disadvantage, and usually pays by the reduction in size or total loss of his territory. Victories are not followed up, and the defeated opponent is allowed to depart - there have been no reports of mortality during territorial fighting.

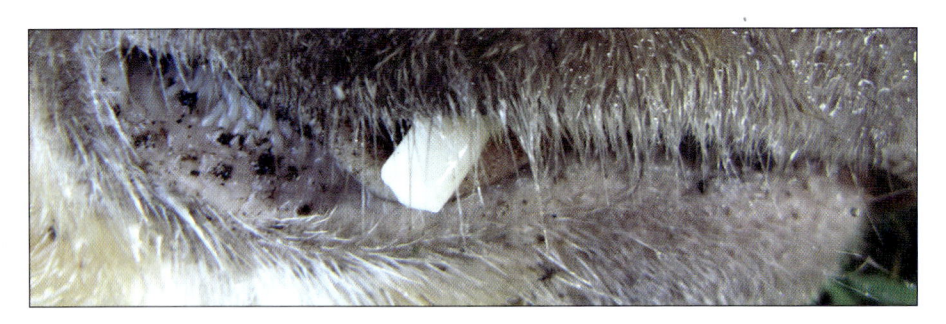

It is quite common for bucks to break their canine tusks, normally during fighting or fraying.

Habitat and Foodstuffs

Muntjac, as we know, are a creature of the undergrowth in their natural habitat, and are loathe to leave dense cover under normal conditions - so much so that muntjac can exist in close proximity to man for years with the latter having little idea of the small deer's presence. As a prey species which can only run in short bursts, they need to have close cover nearby to allow a quick escape. Muntjac are usually reluctant to venture out into open areas except at night.

Muntjac prefer to keep some form of cover close to hand

Any woodland with a dense floor covering is a suitable habitat and bramble thickets provide their most popular strongholds - a relatively low growth will provide for most of their feeding and shelter needs throughout the year. Conifer plantations in their early stages are also preferred, but become less so once they have grown beyond the stage that they offer the cover and security that the muntjac desires. Otherwise any other dense cover can be popular, and overgrown rhododendrons are especially favoured in large suburban gardens and neglected areas of old parks. Gorse will also be readily used if no suitable alternative is available.

Muntjac are a browsing deer and are classified as 'concentrate selectors'. They are physically too small, and their digestive systems not developed sufficiently, to cope with the bulk intake of coarse material. To meet their nutritional needs they need a higher quality of foodstuff that can be quickly processed by their

Rhododendrons provide a popular source of cover and shelter

digestive systems. A deer observed seemingly bulk-feeding grazing on grass is more likely to be carefully selecting new growth among the grasses and herbs. In woodland where numbers get too high, there may be damage to the sub-storey and ground flora such as bluebells, dog's mercury and primroses can suffer heavy damage. In such cases they can cause considerable concern to the environmentalist.

They like variety in their diet. Bramble is a very important food item as it provides something of food value throughout the year. Blackberries are eagerly taken in season, and an animal's stomach can contain little else when they are in abundance. Ivy is also eaten throughout the year and browsed to the height that the muntjac can reach. This 'browse line' is a useful indication of the presence of muntjac, and a heavy one is an especially good indicator of a high population. Interestingly, although muntjac are capable of standing on their rear legs to increase the height at which they can browse, they do not do so as readily as other species of deer.

Whilst muntjac are capable of standing on their hind legs to browse, such behaviour is rarely seen

Seasonal wild crops such as crab apples, fungi, chestnuts and acorns are readily taken advantage of, as are windfall apples and other fruits in orchards. Nut trees seem particularly important to them, both for their leaves and their crop. The vegetable gardener is also a source of seasonal food - runner beans and brassicas appear to be special favourites. When agricultural crops are at their height and provide sufficient cover, muntjac will often become field-living to take advantage of them. Maize is especially popular. In fact the muntjac is remarkably versatile and will take advantage of any opportunity - anything unusual is likely to be sampled. Even pheasant feed bins can become a ready source of food.

Grasses only become an important item in the muntjac's diet during January and February when there is little else available. Herbs are eaten during the summer months. New

Muntjac are quick to sample anything unusual, such as this small sapling

growth on trees and shrubs is also browsed; if a sapling is springy enough, a muntjac will bend it over to within reach by walking up the trunk and bearing it down using the weight of its chest. Considerable damage can be caused to young trees in this way, where the nipping of shoots and buds can stunt or deform growth.

Although muntjac are content to live in young conifer plantations, conifers themselves are rarely eaten and only then if there is nothing else available. A plantation which offers no other foodstuffs is soon abandoned. Although the banks of watercourses are a popular habitat for muntjac, this is mainly because of the feeding opportunities that they offer. A ready supply of water is not critical to them as they derive moisture from their food even though they will drink on occasion, especially in hot or dry weather.

Muntjac seldom drink except in unusually hot or dry weather

Daily Life

As a small deer with a correspondingly small rumen, the muntjac needs to feed frequently. There are five main peaks of feeding activity throughout the day, each period lasting as long as three hours. During this time the animal will be largely on the move around its territory or home range, feeding as it goes and reaffirming its ownership by scent marking and fraying in the case of bucks. It may linger in areas where a particular food source is abundant.

In undisturbed areas muntjac will feed at any time of the day or night, although heavy disturbance may prompt animals to adopt a more nocturnal existence. Moderate weather conditions do not have any effect on the feeding cycle, although animals will lie up during periods of especially heavy wind or rain. They do not seem too affected by cold weather either, but will seek cover if the temperature drops too far below freezing. Under severe conditions, muntjac in this country have been known to seek shelter in sheds and farm buildings.

Moderate rain has no real effect on daily movement or feeding patterns

After feeding sessions, animals will retire to cover to ruminate

When not feeding, muntjac will lie up in cover and chew the cud. Like all ruminants, the freshly eaten food is stored in the first and largest chamber of the four-chambered stomach. Once at rest, the partly digested food is returned to the mouth a bit at a time and ground down by the cheek teeth. Once properly broken down it is returned to the stomach where it is fully digested. In this way the deer is able to extract the full nutritional value of its foodstuffs whilst spending less time actively feeding and exposing itself to potential predators.

Muntjac will not necessarily seek out the same bedding places time after time, although similar areas of cover are favoured. The main criterion is cover where the animal can feel secure. If that cover exists in conjunction with high ground that offers a vantage point, it is often preferred. Bramble beds on the sides of high mounds are popular.

Like most deer, muntjac swim well and are not deterred by slow moving waterways or small bodies of water. They have been observed crossing small lakes even when under no pressure to do so; their approach to water seems to be quite casual and unhurried. Only particularly strong currents are likely to cause them problems.

Unlike some of the other small, solitary deer species, muntjac will indulge in a larger degree of social interaction such as grooming. Both bucks and does will groom each other as well as dependant fawns, leading to the misconception that the buck plays a larger part in the raising of the fawn. This is not so - once it is old enough to do so, it is the doe that the fawn accompanies on feeding bouts. Mutual grooming concentrates around the head and neck, and becomes more intensive during spring when the moult into summer coat is taking place.

Mutual grooming is an important part of daily life.

Breeding Cycle
Unlike all other British deer species, the muntjac has no set breeding season - rutting and birthing can take place at any time of the year. The doe reaches sexual maturity and comes into oestrus for the first time at the age of about seven months, in some cases as young as six. It seems that the actual age is heavily dependant on the doe reaching a threshold body weight, estimated at around 10 kg (22 lbs), which enables the process to begin. In comparison, the buck takes slightly longer to reach sexual maturity, which he achieves at about nine months old and a threshold weight of 12 kg (26 lbs). He will remain fertile all year round thereafter, even when he has cast his antlers or is in velvet.

Bucks remain fertile all year round. This one, in velvet, is pursuing a doe that has just come into season.

Bucks are attracted to does in season by their scent, which she leaves as she travels about her home range. Bucks can be seen actively following scent trails, often seemingly preoccupied to the point that they are far less aware of what is going on around them than normal. This activity may lead them into another buck's territory and it is at such times that aggression between bucks is most likely to take place. Mating follows a short period of the buck pursuing the doe; there is no complex system of displaying or chasing.

The single fawn is born after a gestation period of 210 days - about seven months. Although twin foetuses have been recorded, such instances are so rare as to be virtually non-existent. Within 36 hours of giving birth the doe comes into season again and the process repeats itself. If a successful mating does not take place, the doe will continue to come into season every two weeks until she does conceive. As a result, the muntjac doe will spend the vast majority of

Fawns are no larger than a rabbit when born. Even at this early age, the sub-orbital gland (just in front of the eye) is easily visible and easily distinguishes them from the young of other deer.

Fawns are not fully weaned until they are about two months

A fawn grows fast and is quickly able to accompany its mother.

her adult life pregnant. One animal, which lived to 14 years old in captivity, raised a total of 19 fawns during her lifetime.

Fawn survival rates are high, even during all but the most extreme winter conditions. For their first few days of life they are left lying motionless in cover while their mother feeds, and it is during this time that they are most vulnerable to predators. Fox predation seems to be at its highest during the winter, when there is less cover and the fawn is more easily discovered. Fawns are soon able to accompany their mother on feeding bouts, and are fully weaned by the time that they are around two months old. As this is around the time when they tend to lose their spots, it is fair to assume that any fawn seen with spots is likely to still be fully dependant on its mother.

Reaching sexual maturity so young and not being tied to specific breeding seasons are the key reasons that allow an uncontrolled muntjac population to explode. By the same token, the fact that a mature doe will almost inevitably have a fawn dependent on it to some degree makes the humane management of muntjac a serious challenge. Only by being prepared to cull heavily pregnant does, and thus ensuring that any previous fawn has grown sufficiently to a point of independence, can we begin to have an impact on a growing population while doing so in an ethical manner.

Communication
Scent plays an important part in the daily life of an animal that lives a largely solitary existence in dense cover. The muntjac possesses a number of scent glands on various parts of the body, all of which are used to mark territory, to signal that it has come into season, or simply to identify itself to others of the species within the same area.

The most important glands are the sub-orbital (situated in large sockets immediately in front of each eye) and the frontal glands on the forehead. The sub-orbital glands seem to be capable of being opened at will, and are most frequently opened during courtship or when defecating or urinating; they are important for the scent marking of territories. The frontal glands are most heavily used by the buck and are rubbed on vegetation or directly onto the ground.

The frontal glands are situated on the forehead, directly between the eyes. The sub-orbital glands are directly in front of each eye. Both sets of glands are very obvious on the adult deer.

A further set of glands is contained between the cleaves of the hind feet, and are probably used to leave identifying scent trails for other deer. There are also paired glands located within the pelvis, opening into the urethra in the male and the vagina in the female. It is understood that these glands are unique to the muntjac and, as marking with urine seems especially important to muntjac, it is very likely that they are linked to this activity.

Not for nothing are muntjac also known as the barking deer. They are the most vocal of our deer, and use their single, terrier-like bark or yap (not as deep as that of roe deer) to sound an alarm or a challenge, or to signal their location to other deer. Both sexes bark; does in oestrus are especially vocal. Each bark is repeated every few seconds, and can go on for up to an hour. Otherwise muntjac make a variety of other noises which are not heard so often. A doe hotly pursued by a buck will squeak submissively. Bucks have also been heard to

Both sexes will bark, often carrying on for very long periods

grunt, make a chattering noise and click their teeth. Fawns in danger will squeal, or bleat when separated from their mother. Adult animals in extremis make a loud, distressing scream.

Only bucks seem to indulge in fraying, which can take place anywhere within a territory, not just on the boundaries. The canine tusk or the lower incisors are used to remove the bark of saplings with careful, upwards movements. Wisps of the bark are usually left on the trunk, and are not normally eaten. Once fraying is completed, the bare surface will usually be anointed with scent from the sub-orbital or frontal glands. Usually it is thin saplings - perhaps the diameter of a pen or finger – that seem to be chosen for this activity. Bucks will also make shallow scrapes with their forefeet around their territories - these are anything up to a metre across, and can be made in ground herbage as well as directly into the earth.

Fraying damage to a sapling   *Scrape*

Muntjac have exceptionally long tongues. Here, the sub-orbital gland is moistened as part of a series of alarm gestures which included foot-stamping and barking. The picture is a frame from a digital film, and the action was completed so quickly that it was only noticed when the film was played back slowly.

Whilst naturally curious, the muntjac has various means of signalling alarm to others of its kind in the vicinity. An animal which spots a potential danger will extend its neck as it tries to identify the source of disturbance; often it will stamp hard with its forefoot to make an audible thump. It may also bark at the intruder. If sufficiently alarmed, the tail is raised to vertical, exposing the white underside, before the animal departs - usually at speed.

Tracks, Trails and Signs
In addition to fraying stocks and scrapes, as already described, muntjac leave a number of other signs of their presence. Their tracks are small enough to be confused with those of roe kids during the summer months, though they are unmistakable during the winter. Side by side, the tracks of roe look huge against the daintier slots of muntjac.

The outer cleave of each muntjac hoof has a tendency to be longer than the inner one. In some instances the difference in length is striking, but this is not universal and cannot be relied upon as a means of identification. If the cleaves are splayed in a 'v', the animal was running. If the animal is heavily pregnant, the slots of the hind feet tend to register wider apart than those of the forefeet. Otherwise, because of their size, it is difficult to all but the most experienced observer to read a lot more into muntjac tracks. Their real value to the deer manager is to give a general impression of the animal's presence in, and use of the area.

A muntjac slot alongside a 50p piece

A roe slot for comparison, again next to a 50p piece. Note that the cleaves have spread in a 'V', indicating that the animal was running.

    The muntjac's small size and light weight means that there is often little sign of its passing during the warmer months when the ground is hard and holds few imprints. Runways and tunnels in the undergrowth still give a good indication of its presence. They are just large enough to accommodate the user, and significantly larger than the passageways of rabbits or hares. Some are very heavily used. Trails left in the grass are narrower than might be expected, at little over 10 cm wide.

A well worn muntjac tunnel. These can be more obvious during the summer months when the ground vegetation is denser.

Muntjac droppings are small at about 12mm long. Their appearance is dark, smooth, shiny and firm, and they are oval in shape, coming to a slight point at one end. They are usually separate but will sometimes adhere together in small lumps. Although muntjac will frequently return to the same place to defecate, producing latrine areas, droppings are just as likely to be found scattered along pathways and around popular feeding areas.

Muntjac droppings. Pellets are not always found coalesced like this, but may be scattered in loose groups.

Rabbit and hare droppings in comparison are rounded, brown and fibrous, and it is difficult to confuse the two. Roe deer droppings are very similar in appearance, if slightly larger and longer in the case of adults.

Other signs to look for are cast hair, especially during the spring moult, and particularly on wire and creepways under fences. Mention has already been made of the browse line - the height to which deer feed. In the case of muntjac it is about 60cm (about 2 feet) off the ground, and as high as 85cm if the animal stands on its hind legs. Occasionally it can be even higher than this where the deer has bent over saplings to get at buds and leaves. Care should be taken not to confuse deer damage to plants with that of rabbits and hares. Twigs bitten through by the latter show a clean cut. Deer, having no upper incisors, leave a more ragged edge to the bite.

Mortality

For such a small animal, the muntjac has a remarkably long life-span. Captive animals regularly live up to 16 years, and even in the wild 14 years is not uncommon although 10 is probably more usual. While roe deer populations tend towards self regulation, with over-population frequently resulting in a build up of disease and related deaths, muntjac seem to be more resilient in this respect. They are a very robust little deer. Doubtless their ability to live in closer proximity to each other helps, along with a readier acceptance of smaller territorial needs.

They are also not badly affected by the extremes of the British weather, although prolonged periods of extreme cold cause problems. Animals will be more prone to seek cover and spend more time in it as food becomes in shorter supply. The last big die-off within the UK muntjac population (in 1963) was the result of severe winter conditions which lasted for many weeks, and very high numbers of muntjac (as much as 70% of the estimated population in some places) died as a result. Deep snow is a very real problem; not only does it make it difficult for the animal to forage for food, but restricts it from fleeing from dogs.

Deep snow that persists over long periods can be a significant cause of muntjac mortality.

During periods when food is inaccessible for whatever reason, the muntjac will live off its internal fat reserves. Once these are used up there is little to fall back on, and the animal deteriorates rapidly. Artificial feeding during hard weather is seldom effective; the animal's digestive system simply cannot adjust rapidly enough to the rough forage provided, and animals will often be found dead with full stomachs as a result.

No native British predator is capable of bringing down a mature muntjac. Fawns are a different matter. During their first weeks of life, when they are little larger than a rabbit, they are prey to foxes, cats and badgers. Foxes are without doubt the most significant predator and can take large numbers of fawns. Domestic dogs will chase mature muntjac which, not being capable of sustaining high speeds over long distances, are very vulnerable. The muntjac is not entirely defenceless and will occasionally see off a dog using tusks, antlers and hooves if brought to bay. Serious injuries inflicted by the tusks of bucks, requiring multiple stitches, are occasionally reported by the owners of dogs used to flush pheasants on organised shoots in areas holding muntjac.

One of the biggest killers of British muntjac is the motor car. Countless numbers die on the roads each year, and studies suggest that the males constitute the majority. It is quite possible that territorial behaviour, or younger animals seeking new ranges, might account for this. As I have said, the muntjac is a remarkably robust animal. How many road traffic accident victims are not killed outright and manage to crawl away to die in cover can only be guessed at.

The motor car is a major killer of muntjac

CHAPTER 3
Management Principles

The Need to Cull

Before considering the principles behind the management of muntjac, it is a good idea to understand why we need to do so in the first place. There are many reasons depending on your viewpoint - the forester may be concerned by damage to his young trees, the farmer may consider his crops or the conservationist may regard the loss of bluebell woods or rare orchids with dismay. But at the root of the issue has got to be the welfare of the deer themselves.

No species of deer in this country has a natural predator capable of keeping its numbers in check. True, foxes and loose dogs may account for the occasional fawn, and road traffic accidents kill a good many adults on our roads, but there is no doubt that the muntjac population would increase even more rapidly were it not for human intervention.

The muntjac, as a largely solitary species, can only sustain a certain population level before stresses increase in all directions. An expanding population can quickly reach the point where damage to the environment, conflict with human activities and other native fauna, and the stripping of local resources to the point of starvation become intolerable. Contrary to the belief of some, death from old age is not a common

In Britain, a mature muntjac has no natural predators, Control must therefore fall to man.

process in the natural world; in reality, older animals tend to succumb to predators more easily well before they reach this point. If not, their teeth wear down to the point that foodstuffs cannot be properly broken down and death from malnutrition results. Death from 'old age' is simply a misnomer.

We must not forget that even the muntjac evokes the 'Bambi factor' and that there are those who will always decry the destruction of any one of Britain's larger land mammals even in the face of practical argument. It has

The worn down teeth of an old deer (bottom) against those of a yearling (top). Worn teeth are incapable of breaking down foodstuffs enough for the digestive system to cope with efficiently.

been suggested, quite seriously, that old deer could be fitted with false teeth! Other unlikely solutions to containing the spread of muntjac, such as administering contraceptive drugs, are quite simply impractical for a wild deer population and could have serious effects on other wildlife.

That said, it is foolish to dismiss the sensitivities of a largely well meaning, if misinformed, public. As a result our management of the species must be thoughtful, constructive and humane at all times.

Minimising Damage - Exclusion and Deterrents
Before we look at culling principles in more detail, it is worth examining other means of reducing the impact of deer on our environment. Very often shooting is an inappropriate means of control - say, in heavily built up areas when safety considerations forbid it. Under such circumstances it is necessary to keep muntjac at bay by other means.

Fencing is an option, but it needs to be comprehensive. A muntjac is capable of clearing a barrier five feet high, a considerable feat for such a small and robustly built animal. Chances are, though, that it is more likely to go through or under the obstacle if it can. Any mesh used should be no larger than 75mm (3"). Although 100mm (4") mesh is effective, there is a danger of bucks becoming trapped when their antlers have snagged. Woven or welded square mesh is best and more robust; chain link also works well but is difficult to tension effectively. A scrape under the fence big enough to let a small dog or fox through will accommodate a muntjac, especially when there is some play in the bottom wire. Ideally, the base of the fence should be buried in the ground – it has been suggested that, if the wind can pass under a fence, so can a muntjac!

Electric fences, equipped with a stand-off wire, can be effective in deterring deer but are not so good in the longer term as the deer learn to jump them, or a lack of maintenance renders them ineffective. Avoid at all costs any form of flimsy plastic mesh, electrified or not, as the deer can become entangled with them with disastrous consequences.

A buck captured in full flight. For its size and build, the muntjac is capable of clearing surprisingly high obstacles

A creepway under a link mesh fence; muntjac are capable of getting through even smaller spaces yet

Comprehensive fencing is necessary where large areas of plants need to be protected during the vulnerable stages of growth

Two adjacent, experimental deer exclosures in Norfolk. The one on the left is state-of-the-art electric fencing with strobe lighting and solar panels to recharge the system – muntjac are frequently found feeding within it. On the right is a simple fence of 5' rigid plastic mesh, laid flat for about two feet at the base and covered with earth. Although there are plenty of signs of muntjac trying to push their way through, none have succeeded

Tree guards are effective for more valuable plants in their early stages of growth, and need to be a minimum of 1m high to be effective. Tree tubes or similar seem to be the best solution; spiral plastic tree guards, effective against rabbits, are less so where deer are concerned.

Mechanical deterrents and scarers, such as scarecrows, 'bangs', flashing lights and the like can be very useful, but their effectiveness diminishes as the deer get used to them. Noise makers may well attract complaints in residential areas! A useful ploy that some gardeners have found effective is a cheap transistor radio, set to any 'talk' station and left to play quietly during the hours of darkness. It is the human voices that deter the deer – music does not have the same effect.

Protective tree tubes must be high enough to be effective. The plant within this short tube has been browsed down by deer every time that new growth has emerged.

Commercial chemical deer repellents exist, but their effects are limited and tend to be short-term. Great care needs to be exercised when plants are in a rapid growth cycle, as the repellent can actually kill them. All chemical repellents (including bags of human hair and lion dung, both reported to be effective where available!) come under very stringent regulations for their use.

In areas where road traffic accidents are a problem, it is possible to erect reflective posts which warn the deer of approaching vehicles. Signs can warn motorists of the presence of deer and persuade them to reduce speed, but drivers quickly tend to ignore them if they do not regularly see actual animals crossing. Other devices are available, but the only method that has proven 100% effective has been comprehensive, well maintained roadside fencing with underpasses for the deer where necessary. Otherwise, as a bare minimum, roadside verges should be kept short to allow deer and drivers visibility of each other and be able to exercise caution. Dense vegetation right up to the roadside is a death trap as far as deer are concerned.

Public Considerations

Like it or not, we live in a largely urban society with urban values. To many, meat in its natural state comes wrapped in cling film from Tescos rather than in fur or feathers. Walt Disney taught us years ago that animals not only talk to each other (in English) but have human values and reactions as well. Animals exist for humans to look at, cuddle, and 'rescue' when they fall into difficulties. This is not, for the most part, the fault of the public – it is a reflection of the times we live in, and the fact that people are becoming more and more detached from the realities of the natural world.

It is astonishing that a society that accepts television images of lions despatching wildebeest on the Serengeti (usually at tea time, and in close-up!) can express outrage when the culling of British fauna has to take place to keep things in balance. We must be practical - killing to survive is part of the natural balance. It keeps populations in check and if nature is not placed to do so, man has to become the predator before numbers grow to the point when the environment can no longer support them and disaster results.

The deer manager has to operate in the face of a great many misconceptions. Whilst he appreciates the realities and reasons for what he is doing, many others will not. We will never totally overcome this, but through a process of discretion, education and sympathy for the views of others - whether we find them misguided or not - we can at least reach a state of truce and, if we are lucky, create converts.

An increase in leisure use of the British countryside increases the chances of conflict between visitor and stalker. More and more people are looking to rural pursuits, ranging from rambling to mountain-biking, as their escape from city life for a brief period of recreation. The 'Right to Roam' will further increase public access to places where, before, rural activities could take place without the danger of upsetting delicate sensibilities. The stalker has to accept this and work around it.

Discretion is the key. Although you may feel that your camouflage suit and face mask are necessary for success, consider the effect that the well-dressed stalker has on the family walking down a public footpath (especially when he is carrying a rifle, or, worse yet, a dead Bambi). If contact with the public is unavoidable while stalking, take off your face mask and gloves, conceal any carcase you may be carrying and lay your rifle on the ground before greeting them.

The stalker must take special care to avoid conflict with other land users

Think too of your gralloch, and how you dispose of it. Even the bloodstained patch of ground where it was conducted may cause the person who stumbles upon it to leap the most lurid conclusions! Grallochs are best conducted well away from public areas, and disposed of carefully. If the stalker thinks about what he is doing and the image that he presents, he vastly reduces the potential for conflict and misplaced outrage.

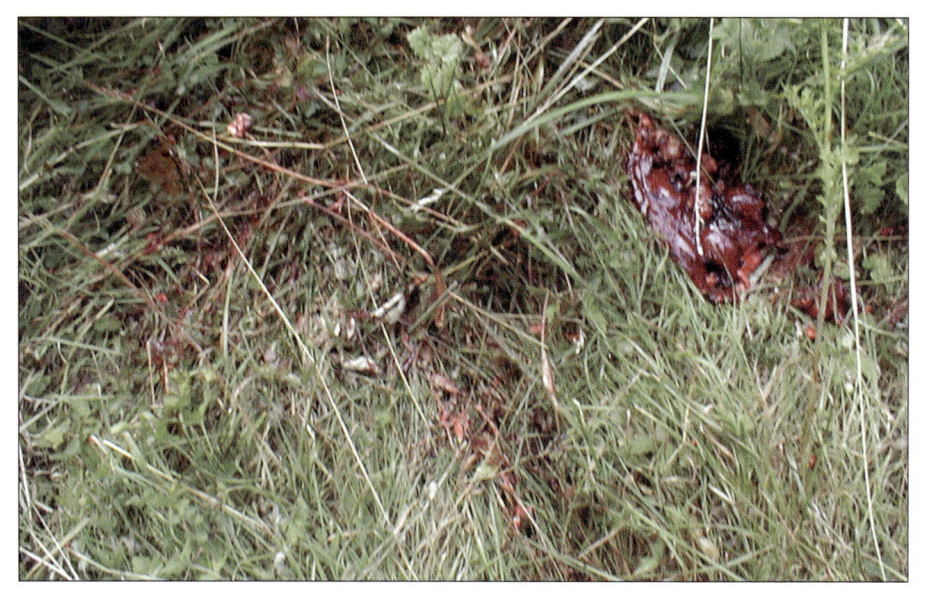

Consider how the aftermath of a gralloch would seem to an unsuspecting walker

Always take any opportunity to educate people in the reasons for deer management. You will be surprised at how many are receptive. People, brought up on a diet of raw Disney, are often impressed when someone takes the trouble to explain realities. The 'if it's brown it's down' approach to deer management is counter productive, and does no good to the humane and intelligent approach that you must present.

Think, too, about your fellow land users. It is a rare stalker who has the exclusive use of a piece of ground. Farmers, foresters, gamekeepers and a host of others have a job to do. If you take the trouble to get to know them, explain what you are doing and show that you are keen to deconflict your activities, you will be going a long way towards making useful allies. Such people, in the course of their work, will see deer on a regular basis and can rapidly become extra sets of 'eyes and ears' working on your behalf.

Above all, your watchword must be safety. Never forget that you are privileged to be allowed to use a lethal weapon as you go about your business. We live on an overcrowded island and people do not always respect private land and stick to public rights of way. Tragedies cannot be undone, and your ownership and use of a firearm demands an exceptional degree of trust by society as a whole. Always be conscious of where a bullet may end up, and if in any doubt don't shoot. Your actions have to be irreproachable, ethically and legally, at all times.

It can take a lifetime to build a reputation, but an instant to destroy it.

Urban Challenges
Discussion of relations with the public at large leads neatly onto the challenges that urban or semi-urban deer populations pose the stalker. Of all the deer species, muntjac are the most likely to tuck themselves away in the oddest places and can become especially tolerant of the close proximity of man. Like the fox, they have proven exceptionally adaptable to a lifestyle on the urban fringe. However, unlike the fox, which is frequently trapped and relocated from city areas, their presence goes largely unnoticed and they are, where it is, mostly tolerated. After all, most people like to see deer.

Such deer can become noticeably nonchalant about the presence of humans as long as they have suitable cover to retire to. They are quick to learn what is a threat and what is not, and many a gardener can vouch for this. It is here that urban problems tend to occur - deer and human activities frequently do not mix, and the stalker may be asked to do something about damage or the potential for road traffic accidents.

Firearms and built up areas are a dangerous combination. First and foremost is the safety aspect of shooting near dwellings, and it is a foolish stalker who attempts to solve a gardener's problems under such circumstances. Add to that the disturbance factor of high velocity shots and the sensitivity of members of the public and you quickly realize that the whole business is a minefield. It is most sensible in such cases to politely decline the request, and refer the person to their local council.

Firearms certificates are usually very proscriptive on where the weapons held may be used, and the quickest way to lose one is to step outside the rules. The words 'places deemed suitable by the Chief Constable' tend to be included in the wording on the most open of conditions for use of a particular firearm. So if you are invited to solve a deer problem in a place close to human habitation, even if you consider shooting to be safe, it is a wise move to consult the local police for their approval first.

Occasionally an animal will become 'trapped' in an area, usually fenced off, which is a patently unsuitable place for it to be. Unless the animal is clearly distressed, it is best left undisturbed. You will usually find that it wanders out the way that it got in. Don't be too tempted to get yourself involved if it needs to be moved; local vets or zoo staff are usually better experienced and trained for darting or live capture. On no account should attempts be made to drive a wild deer out of an enclosed area; the creature will inevitably panic and stands a strong chance of damaging itself trying to escape

Muntjac can get through the smallest gaps and often appear to be trapped in enclosed areas; left in peace, they will normally find their own way out

If you do find yourself shooting close to occupied buildings, have a thought to the effect that the sound of high velocity shots may have on the inhabitants. One muffled bang at five o'clock in the morning may wake someone enough to wonder what it was, but it takes two to alert them to the fact that shooting is going on. In such cases, the fitting of a sound moderator to your rifle is a good move and reduces the potential for alarm and concern.

In heavily built up areas where deer have become a problem, shooting is out of the question for management purposes. The only options are exclusion or physical removal of the animals. Fencing and similar measures are inevitably expensive, and need to be done properly if they are to be 100% effective. Trapping and other methods of capturing live deer require a special license and are best left to the experts. Of course, if the garden concerned has a basic fence, you can always suggest a free-roaming dog to persuade the deer to raid elsewhere!

Census Techniques, Acceptable Densities and a Balanced Population
How many muntjac have you actually got on your ground?   Even to get a rough idea is an art rather than a science - we are dealing with a secretive creature that favours thick undergrowth, rather than one which readily shows itself and stands still to be counted. Quite often, the most we can hope for is a 'best guess'. Of all our deer species, muntjac are the most difficult to count. It usually a fair bet that for every one you actually see, there are another dozen hidden away in the near vicinity.

Forget the techniques such as hill counts, which establish a number of observers to record what they see over a set time period and collate results at the end of the day. Only two methods are likely to come close to being effective - dung counts and driven counts.

The dung count is a method beloved of many researchers to determine the numbers of deer in a given area. It does not involve physically counting the deer themselves, but instead samples measured plots of ground for dung pellets. The whole process is very time consuming and I suspect that the vast majority stalkers are unwilling to go to such lengths.

Driven counts, where the geography of the ground permits it, may be possible. The ground is driven towards observers who, within sight of each other, record each deer that passes them. Smaller sections of an overall patch of woodland might be driven and counted, then multiplied by the whole to get an indicative figure of deer present. Beware, though - deer are not co-operative in such matters and tend to go in any direction but the one that you want! Also, if not driven effectively, muntjac are particularly prone to stay put and let the beaters walk past them.

There is a simpler way of getting an idea of how many deer your ground holds. Use your eyes, and spend time out there. Keep a record of the sexes and age categories you see, and look for trends. Speak to people such a gamekeepers, farmers and foresters who know the ground. Consider the occasional night sortie armed with a spotlight. Over a period of time you will build up an impression of your deer population. If, next year, you start to see more animals, the population is probably increasing. If you see less, it is probably decreasing.

My point is this - *you cannot accurately count muntjac.* You can, however, create a impression in your own mind of what you have got.

The habits and habitat of muntjac do not lend themselves to easy or accurate counting

If attempting to count muntjac is largely ineffective under most normal circumstances, there is no point in being tempted to produce a more than a simple outline cull plan. The habits and visibility of the other deer species allow a much more involved approach. Cull selection and criteria are dealt with below; an acceptable density of muntjac for your area is quite simply one which minimises conflict with human activities, and just as importantly ensures that the deer population remains healthy, viable and in balance with the environment. Try not to think in numbers – you will only end up misleading yourself. Think, rather, in terms of 'one or two,' 'a few', 'quite a few' or 'lots'. Vague, perhaps, but far more practical. If you are seeing a few animals on your ground, the unseen ones will probably add up to a fair sized population. If you are seeing quite a few or lots, chances are that it is time to take some serious action and get those numbers reduced.

Acceptable densities of animals will vary according to local circumstances. One very experienced deer professional tells me that he would happily see over a hundred muntjac in a square kilometre of woodland that is rich in suitable forage and cover, whereas lesser ground might only hold a fraction of that number comfortably. Numbers drop as the quality of habitat decreases. By and large, an area that would comfortably hold fifty roe would accommodate twice the number of muntjac – but not both, of course. In the end, an acceptable density of deer is a local decision based on any number of factors. If the woodland understorey is disappearing, deer road traffic accidents are up, carcase weights are down, gardeners are complaining about damage or - more alarmingly - you start to find deer carcasses in the woods, you have probably got too many muntjac and it is time to do something about it.

A browse line on a field edge, showing where muntjac have systematically foraged a hedgerow over a period of time.

In an ideal world you are seeing as many bucks as does, the majority of animals that you shoot are in the young to early-middle age groups, and you are not finding animals dead during the winter. You see a few animals on each outing, but do not trip over one every time you turn a corner, and a visit to your ground at night does not show up groups of animals feeding together like so many rabbits. Your deer population is healthy with predictable carcase weights, carries moderate levels of external parasites (ticks, keds and the like) and very few signs of internal parasites. Evidence of disease is rare to the point of almost non-existent. There are few signs of territorial aggression, beyond the inevitable signs of normal fighting between bucks, damage levels to the environment are acceptable to all interests, and only the occasional animal is killed on the road.

If this is so you can reasonably assume that you have a fairly well-balanced muntjac population. Consider yourself fortunate, get cracking and keep it that way!

The ultimate aim of management is a balanced and healthy deer population

Cull Selection

The dictionary definition of *cull* is to pick or select. Before we go any further, it is worth holding that thought. We are not talking about sport hunting in its own right - although that may indeed have a place within a cull plan. We are being selective in what we shoot, and doing it for good reasons. That said, it is very difficult (though not impossible) to overshoot a muntjac population, and you have to take your chances where they are offered - within reason.

We have already seen that the muntjac, unlike our other deer species, is completely aseasonal in its breeding habits and as a result it is impossible to specify times when it is possible to cull females without the risk of orphaning a dependant fawn. This is the main challenge of culling muntjac. Furthermore, the stalker is faced by a restless quarry which does not lend itself to prolonged observation. So there is little time to mull over whether to shoot or not - he has to make a rapid decision and act upon it in the time available or the opportunity will be lost.

Be wary of culling a mature doe that is being hotly pursued by a buck. Very likely she has just given birth and come into oestrus again.

As muntjac are not protected by close seasons what then, should we shoot? The British Deer Society recommends that only heavily pregnant and obviously immature does should be culled to reduce the risk of orphaning. This puts the onus firmly on the stalker to be completely familiar with the appearance of his quarry.

Body size is a good start, but muntjac grow quickly and are approaching adult proportions by the time they are only eight months old. A 'chubby', short face is a good indicator of an immature animal in addition to smaller size in comparison with the adult - as the adult jawbone with a full complement of teeth develops, the face of the adult doe becomes long and tapering.

Regrettably, we must accept the probability of shooting a high proportion of heavily pregnant does if we follow this policy. The truth of the matter is that controlling numbers of females is the key to controlling the overall population. You can shoot as many bucks as you like but this will not keep the population in check, even if it may reduce local damage levels to some degree. To discover a well-developed foetus when conducting the gralloch may be distasteful, but it is a sure sign that there is not a dependent fawn hidden away somewhere. The latter, if it is not lucky enough to fall prey to a fox, has no future but to succumb to starvation or the elements. By the same token, shooting a youngster that has barely lost its spots can be equally distasteful. Sadly, in areas with an excessive muntjac population, you will need to harden your heart and do just that if you are to stand a chance of reducing numbers effectively.

Two pregnant does – the frontmost is at a very advanced stage of pregnancy and could be culled with no risk of orphaning a dependant fawn.

This doe has only just given birth and is noticeably thin

It is much easier to select bucks for culling as they play no part in the raising of fawns. Broadly speaking, they can be shot as seen. The decision to pass up a buck - perhaps, where a specific trophy to hang on the wall is sought - is itself a luxury confined to areas where there is not heavy pressure to cull large numbers for control purposes. Even when the antlers have been cast, the long pedicles make positive identification of a mature buck a simple matter.

Although muntjac territories tend to be small in comparison with other species such as roe deer, and bucks tend to be more tolerant of each other throughout the year, do give some thought to preserving any particularly dominant specimen that you may have. He will act as a 'policeman' in keeping smaller bucks out of his area, especially if there are a number of doe territories intersecting his. This will reduce feeding and fraying damage in the immediate vicinity, and is an important consideration if this is an important local reason for culling.

Effective culling concentrates on does and younger bucks; trophy animals should not be a priority

It is a good job that judging an animal's age 'on the hoof' does not have the importance in culling muntjac as it does for other species. Once an animal is mature this can be a tricky business. However, points to look for are a heavier build with a more solid rump (especially in bucks), a more deliberate gait and a pronounced sagging of the belly as the animal gets older. Take care not to confuse the latter indicator with pregnancy in does! An understanding of the growth cycle of antlers (as described in Chapter 2) can be a great help in ageing the younger age classes of bucks.

It is much simpler with a dead animal in front of you; an examination of tooth wear will give you a good idea of age for your records. As time progresses, it is a good idea to keep a 'jaw board', holding examples of different ages and wear, for future reference and comparison. Don't forget that tooth wear can vary considerably between localities, depending on the grittiness of the soil and types of forage, both of which will have a distinct bearing on how fast teeth wear down. A middle-aged animal from a place where the food plants are tough and liable to be coated with grit may experience greater tooth wear than one from an area with much easier feeding.

Basic Stalker Training

In considering the reasons for culling, and the need to be selective in what we shoot, it is clear that the stalker needs to know what he is doing. At the most basic level he has to be aware that he is using a high velocity weapon with a lethal range of over two miles, so safety must be paramount. He must be able to identify his quarry and cull within guidelines, accurately and humanely, then ensure that the carcase enters the human food chain without any danger of contamination. On top of this he needs a thorough understanding of his quarry and stalking techniques that will help him to do his job properly. Books (like, I hope, this one) are helpful, but nothing beats one-to-one instruction and practical experience.

The practical guidance of an experienced stalker is invaluable to a newcomer

The DSC1 course offers a practical blend of theoretical and practical stalker training. It ensures that the successful student understands his quarry and can cull it safely, humanely and efficiently.

An experienced stalker willing to teach the novice is the best start that he can get. To find someone willing to take you on is a gift beyond price, as woodland stalkers tend to be solitary types who achieve their best results stalking alone. They are very aware that two people - especially when one is a novice - tend to make the noise of ten! However, to be set on your way by such a person, who will then be on hand to offer advice and guidance, as well as rectify inevitable mistakes, is invaluable. If you receive the offer of such mentorship, appreciate it fully and grab it with both hands. If you pay for your stalking, as many do, take the opportunity to question the professional at every opportunity.

Failing a personal mentor, courses are available all over the country for the novice (or more experienced) stalker. To be sure of a high standard and nationally recognised qualification, the Deer Stalking Certificate Level 1 (DSC1) is strongly recommended. It is run under the arrangements of the British Deer Society, British Association for Shooting and Conservation and other recognised organisations (contacts and addresses can be found in the appendices) and, over the course of several days, provides a thorough introduction to all essential aspects of deer stalking. At the end of the course the student will emerge with a first-class grounding in subjects such as the natural history of deer, stalking equipment and technique, carcase preparation, safety and practical marksmanship. The DSC1 course is, although not mandatory in this country, an excellent start for anyone new to stalking.

Having achieved the DSC1 qualification, this can be built on by completing the next level, DSC2. This certificate is based on practical assessment, typically involving the culling of three deer (of any species) under the supervision of an accredited witness. It is not especially demanding, and simply seeks to establish that the stalker is competent in the practical aspects of stalking, shooting and subsequent carcase handling.

DSC1 and DSC2 have a value that goes beyond the basic training of a novice stalker. They set a solid foundation on which experience and further study can build, putting the novice on the right path from the beginning. To the landowner, who has his own responsibilities for duty of care, they provide a basic proof of competence which is essential in this age of litigation. It is no accident that more and more landowners are demanding that those who would stalk on their land can produce a DSC before they will permit it.

I urge the novice stalker - do not be tempted to go it alone! Seek training of some nature before you set out in pursuit of deer. It will save you a great deal of frustration, and minimise the chances of committing a distressing, wasteful or potentially fatal error.

Legal & Illegal Practices
All British deer - be they truly native or introduced - are protected by the law,

and the muntjac is no different. The only aspect where the muntjac (and, for that matter, the Chinese Water deer at present) lack any legal protection is the absence of a statutory close season.

The law relating to deer is not especially complex but it is fairly exhaustive. The appendices contain suggestions for suitable reading. It is essential to have a good working knowledge - ignorance of the law, it is often said, is no defence and at the very least is likely to cost you your right to own and use a firearm.

There are three vital aspects of deer law that demand special mention. Firstly, under normal circumstances deer may not be shot during the hours of darkness, namely one hour after sunset and one hour before sunrise. This applies across the whole of the United Kingdom. Secondly, as the law stands, you need to hold a Game License before you can shoot deer.

Thirdly, the law specifies minimum requirements for firearms permitted to be used on deer. In England and Wales the rifle must have a calibre of not less than .240", and a muzzle energy of not less than 1,700 foot pounds. In Scotland and Northern Ireland the rules are slightly different, but these areas do not support muntjac populations (yet). It is worth remembering that, as the range of the muntjac creeps northwards, although Scottish law does not specify a minimum calibre, it does demand a bullet of at least 100 grains, muzzle velocity of 2,450 feet per second and muzzle energy of not less than 1,750 foot pounds. Lesser requirements are specified for roe deer - but only roe.

It is widely agreed that many calibres popular for fox control, such as the .223 and .222 families of cartridges, are ideal for muntjac as well as the other smaller deer species. With the right bullet weight and design, most of them would be highly efficient and produce little meat damage, and sporadic moves are being made towards legalisation. However, do not be tempted in the meantime - you would be in breach of the law.

The use of shotguns on deer of any species is a thorny subject which always encourages debate. True, under special circumstances, there are times when the law permits it but for day-to-day management a rifle is a must for both legal and ethical reasons. It is much more difficult to be sure of a humane kill with a shotgun. Before woodland roe stalking became established as best practice in this country, it was common to hear of roe drives being held on many estates. The number of animals that escaped, horrendously maimed in the long term or to suffer a painful and lingering death can only guessed at and deplored. This was one of the driving forces behind the introduction of the Deer Act of 1963, which finally accorded a degree of protection and demanded a more humane approach to deer control.

Today, sadly, it is becoming apparent that shotgun drives are being held - many of which are quite possibly illegal - to reduce muntjac numbers in some places. I do not agree with this practice for a number of reasons. One is that it is impossible to shoot selectively when faced by a fleeting target in cover. Just as importantly, anyone who advocates a shotgun for the humane killing of muntjac should be invited to skin a buck and examine the thickness of the skin on the animal's neck. As a creature that uses razor-sharp canine teeth to fight, it comes as no surprise to note that they are virtually armour-plated and subsequently difficult to kill with shot. A rifle bullet is a far more effective and humane alternative.

Considering its size, the muntjac is a remarkably robust little deer. It follows that we must use the most appropriate means of control if it is to be effective and humane.

Just as there are those who would seek to eradicate muntjac on their land, there are others who want to introduce them for any number of purposes. There have been many reports of animals turning up well away from the main centres of population in this country, some as far away as Aviemore in Scotland and the Lleyn Peninsula of west Wales, and it is impossible to see how they could do so without human help. There are only so many zoos and private collections for muntjac to escape from, and deliberate introduction is an inevitable conclusion.

Some see the muntjac as a sporting quarry for legitimate stalking, whilst other purposes are much more sinister. Stories abound of muntjac being trapped in the Midlands and taken north for illegal coursing with dogs. Even putting aside the ethics of such practices, the live capture of wild deer (for example by netting, trapping or darting) is prohibited without a specific license. In addition, the deliberate introduction or translocation of non-indigenous species is now illegal. Even rehabilitators of animals which have received veterinary treatment must be licensed, and are not allowed to release the animal outside a kilometre of where it was first caught, and then only within twelve named counties.

A word on road traffic accidents (RTAs) is appropriate at this point, especially where the police are becoming increasingly dependent on local deer managers to assist them. First and foremost, a live wild deer is the property of no man, and only becomes so when it is 'rendered into possession' by killing. It then becomes the property of the owner of the land on which it falls. Therefore a motorist who runs over a deer has no claim against the landowner for damage to his car - but the landowner is the technical owner of the carcase (by the same token, if you shoot a deer which runs onto land where you do not have the right to stalk, you are technically stealing if you move to retrieve it without getting permission first).

In an age where 'rescuing animals' is a popular theme of television programmes, there is a common public perception that a deer hit by a car can be taken away and put right by a vet before release. Such cases are sadly rare. It makes my blood boil to see footage of a badly injured deer lying in a ditch, normally attended by a well-meaning rescuer, waiting for a vet to arrive, or being bundled into a car to be driven to a surgery. Deer are wild animals, and the scent and close proximity of human beings terrifies them. A deer that is incapable of fleeing such things is highly unlikely to be merely stunned - the chances are that, despite a lack of external damage, it is suffering from massive internal injuries. The most merciful relief in such circumstances is euthanasia, as quickly as possible to minimise suffering.

A word of caution is timely at this point. I have heard of several instances where vets have been called out to destroy injured deer by lethal injection - then the carcase has been left at the side of a road to be removed in due course. Needless to say, there are members of the public who will not pass up such an obvious (and free) supply of meat and the carcase has disappeared by the time someone has arrived to collect it. To my knowledge, there have been no human fatalities in this country as a result, but any such carcase must be disposed of (preferably by incineration) as quickly as possible to avoid a potential tragedy.

If you find yourself called out to put a deer injured in an RTA out of its misery, do your best to have a policeman in attendance. He will be able to keep the public (and probably a distraught motorist) at a distance as well as ensure that traffic is controlled if necessary. Tell him clearly what you intend to do, and get his agreement before you do it, and ensure that he provides you with an Incident Number for future reference . As we have already seen, if the deer is on private land it would be best to get permission from the owner before entering it to dispatch the animal. Finally, remember that the carcase is not your property, even though you will probably be asked to dispose of it. In my experience, deer killed in RTAs are good for little else but dog food even if they are not too badly smashed up by the impact of a speeding vehicle. The kennels of the local hunt are often appreciative of such offerings. In the eyes of the law, you are committing an offence if you try to sell the carcase to a game dealer as the deer has not been killed by legal means.

A word of warning on the best method of dispatch for an injured deer. Whilst it is perfectly legal to use a shotgun of any gauge for the purpose, a rifle must be of the calibre prescribed by law. As a result, a suppressed .22 rimfire, although ideal for point-blank euthanasia (especially when in close proximity to the public or built up areas), is currently illegal. A knife, properly used, is effective and quiet, but the technique needs to demonstrated to you by someone who knows what they are doing. If you do use a firearm, take special care to ensure that there is a suitable surface behind the deer to catch the bullet, and beware of the potential for ricochets.

The BDS and BASC co-publish an excellent booklet of guidelines for dealing with deer RTAs.

CHAPTER 4
Equipment

Calibres and Bullets

Any calibre of rifle that is legal for the shooting of deer in the UK will humanely kill a muntjac. The law in England and Wales specifies a calibre of not less than .240", and a minimum muzzle energy of 1,700 foot pounds. Every stalker has his favourite calibre, and all have their good points. It is not my intention here to blind the reader with science, simply to offer some food for thought on the selection of the right one for you and to keep things as uncomplicated as possible.

Of course, it is unlikely that you will wish only to shoot muntjac, and the trick is to settle on a calibre that will meet all your needs. If your quarry species is to be restricted to the smaller species of British deer, and perhaps a degree of fox control, the choice is relatively simple. If you want a rifle that will cope with a wider variety of game, you will need to give more serious thought to the matter.

Before choosing a rifle, you must first decide on the calibre that best suits your purposes

The 'entry level' commercial deer calibre for our purposes is the .243 Winchester. It will fire bullets in weights of up to 105 grains, and has the reputation of being 'flat shooting' (that is to say, it has a shallower trajectory than some of the larger, slower calibres). I have even come across commercially-produced cartridges loaded with 125 grain bullets, but unless your rifle is constructed with the right amount of barrel twist you will find that accuracy drops off alarmingly - these are specialist rounds intended for specifically designed 'sniper' barrelled rifles.

The .243 is enormously popular among British stalkers, and with good reason. It is capable, in the right hands, of accounting for any deer that you are likely to meet in this country, although something a bit heavier is preferable for an adrenaline-filled red or sika stag, or fallow buck, during the rut. It is certainly more than sufficient for the diminutive muntjac. Rifles in this calibre have the advantage of light weight and relatively low recoil, an important consideration for a newcomer to rifle shooting.

Another highly popular calibre is the .308 Winchester, the civilian version of the 7.62mm NATO military round. The cartridges are in fact exactly the same dimensions as those of the .243 Winchester, but with a wider neck to accommodate the bigger bullet. It is arguably more versatile; bullet sizes go up to 180 grains and the range available make it suitable for any deer. If you intend to travel on the Continent and shoot wild boar (which are themselves becoming well established in some parts of this country after reintroduction), this is a suitable calibre - the .243 is certainly not up to the job.

A great advantage of the .308 Winchester is its military equivalent. Commercial ammunition is expensive (anything between 80p and £1 per round at the time of writing). Military surplus 7.62 mm ammunition is available on the civilian market at significantly lower cost. Although it is not suitable for shooting deer, being fully jacketed and not designed to expand (it is a paradox that bullets demanded by the Geneva Convention for shooting people are deemed inhumane and illegal for the shooting of deer), it is a cheap alternative which enables you to get more practice on the range while keeping the costs down. A word of warning though - there are several different 7.62 calibres around. The equivalent of the .308 Winchester is 7.62 NATO (7.62 x 51mm). Others have different cartridge case lengths, and will not mix!

A third highly popular calibre is the .270. Like the .308, it is available in a much wider range of bullet weights and is thus more versatile than the .243. It does have something of a reputation for being excessively noisy and having a punishing recoil, but of course that depends heavily on the cartridge load that you are using - and who you are talking to!

In fact, put any number of experienced stalkers together and you will inevitably end up with a debate over which calibre is the best. The truth is that it's a personal choice. If you attend a DSC1 course without your own rifle you will have the opportunity to shoot as part of the course with a borrowed weapon. Another good way of determining what is right for you is to attend a gun club registered guest day and talk to people, hopefully having the opportunity to fire different calibres yourself. These are run by any number of gun clubs or the regional branches of national organisations such as the BDS or BASC.

A selection of popular modern cartridges for deer. From left to right: .22LR (for comparison only), .243 Winchester, .308 Winchester, 6.5x55 Swedish, .270 Winchester, 30-06.

There are plenty of other popular stalking calibres, all of which are just as suitable for muntjac. The bottom line is that a correctly-placed bullet from any deer-legal calibre will effectively kill a muntjac. Many newcomers make the mistake of assuming that larger bullets are more effective - this is not necessarily so. A gut shot animal is just as likely to travel long distances whatever it has been hit with. With such a small, mobile target as a muntjac, accuracy is the name of the game. Any bullet which meets the legal requirement is more than adequate for muntjac if properly placed. That placement is down to you. Ex-servicemen whose military training has included the use of full bore weapons have few problems in this respect, but some of the larger calibres can be a little daunting to the newcomer.

My personal choice is the .243 Winchester. Over the years I have used this calibre for all species of British deer and experienced no significant problems with it although, for the deliberate stalking of sika and red deer - and for practice on the range - I also own a .308. Occasionally the .243 does not deliver enough energy at the target end to produce sufficient shock to immediately knock down a large deer, even if it might be technically dead on its feet, and long search for the animal can result even if it has expired quickly after running a few yards in thick cover. I prefer to find the animal dead on the spot where it was standing when hit. So, my suggestion for the person whose bread and butter is likely to be muntjac, roe and longer-range fox control is a .243. A .308 is a more versatile compromise if larger game is likely to be on the menu.

I have found that on the occasions I have shot muntjac with a .308, carcase damage has been somewhat greater but there is not a lot of meat to damage at the front end of it anyway. I treat whatever I can salvage from the forelegs and neck as a bonus. There is a school of thought that suggests that, by utilising a slower and heavier bullet for small deer (say, a 180 grain .308 bullet instead of the more usual 150 grain) meat damage is reduced. From what I have seen this certainly seems to have some truth in it.

Do take care when choosing a calibre to ensure that the ammunition for it is readily available. There are a lot of obsolete ones out there and, unless you reload your own ammunition, you may quickly find that you run into supply problems. Also take special care to ensure that the ammunition is the right match for the rifle. Although the family of .22 full bore variants (including the .222, 22-250 and .223) are not legal for use on any deer in England and Wales, there is a growing movement towards amending this aspect of the law. None of these are interchangeable, nor are some of the Continental cartridges whose designations can be very similar. Putting the wrong cartridge into a rifle can radically reduce accuracy in the best case, and produce catastrophic results in the worst.

Many stalkers find reloading their own ammunition a natural progression from shooting with expensive commercial rounds. Not only can costs be cut by as much as three-quarters, but accuracy can also be greatly enhanced as loads are tailored to individual rifles. Reloading is a great advantage to the stalker, and although it is a relatively simple process, great care needs to be taken as the margins for error are very narrow indeed. The novice should always seek guidance from someone who knows what they are doing, or attend a course run by experts. The BDS and BASC, among others, run such courses.

Rifles
Once you have decided what calibre you need, now for the rifle itself. Of all the types available - single shot, double barrels, underlevers etc - it is no surprise that most stalkers opt for the good old-fashioned bolt action rifle. It is a robust, reliable and accurate type of action proven by time and experience, and has the added advantage of being relatively inexpensive to produce. The stalker also has the advantage of a reservoir of ammunition held within the magazine of the rifle itself, and reloading is quickly and simply done with a swift backwards and forwards movement of the bolt.

You can spend as much or as little as you want (or can afford). A custom, hand-made rifle of the finest materials, fitted to you personally, can cost many thousands of pounds. An off-the-shelf, mass-produced one will only be a few hundred. Both will be capable of producing high degrees of accuracy.

A classic design of stalking rifle; bolt action, walnut stock and blued barrel

You do not need to spend a fortune to acquire a suitable stalking rifle. This Brno .308 is well over twenty years old and has had several owners. It remains a reliable workhorse that still shoots as straight as the day that it left the factory. A visit to a reputable dealer can find you a similar bargain if you are working to a strict budget.

You may find the choice of design bewildering at first. Wooden or synthetic stocks, light or heavy barrels, carbines or full length - the list goes on. Much falls to personal preference but in the end you are looking for a tool suited to the task. Firstly, you need a practical rifle for use at stalking ranges, not a long-distance snipers weapon. Most of your shooting will be done at ranges of 100 metres or less. You therefore do not need a heavily barrelled weapon designed for great accuracy at longer distances. More important to the stalker's purposes is a light, manageable weapon that can be brought to bear on a target quickly and shoot accurately.

The carbine or the fullstock (also known as stutzen) rifle, with its woodwork extending to the end of the barrel, can be very tempting. Having a shorter barrel (around 20 inches as opposed the more usual 24 inches) they are much lighter, quick-handling and easier to use in cover. Although a shorter barrel does reduce muzzle velocity slightly, this is not an issue at deer stalking ranges. The light barrel associated with a fullstock rifle may reduce overall weight, but as a result it also overheats quickly after a few shots with a corresponding effect on accuracy and zero - not an issue in the field, but a disadvantage where prolonged range work is taking place.

Stutzen, or fullstock, rifles are a delight to handle but have some disadvantages.

A short rifle may also increase the problem of muzzle blast, which extends backwards and sideways. This may well lead to flinching problems among inexperienced shooters. The wood of the stock must also be of high quality and properly cured, unlike the kiln-dried stocks of mass-produced rifles. If not, it may tend to warp once damp - with disastrous effects on accuracy. The area of stock that needs to 'float' from the barrel is greater and hence has to be kept clear of twigs and other debris, or accuracy can once again be affected. In short the stutzen is a very attractive and useful rifle, but the beginner should think long and hard before going for one.

A practical stalking rifle with a synthetic stock and stainless steel barrel, fitted with a sound moderator

The traditional stalking rifle is constructed with a 'blued' steel barrel and wooden stock and can be prone to rust and warping if not properly cared for. Whilst admittedly less attractive, modern materials are much more practical. Stocks are now available in synthetic materials, and barrels in stainless steel – a huge advantage worth looking hard at.

Above all, make sure that the rifle fits you as an individual. A rifle that suits the person firing it is inevitably going to be more accurate than one which is too long or too short, or which does not come into the aiming position comfortably for whatever reason. The adage 'try before you buy' couldn't be more true. Although stocks can be extended or shortened, it makes more sense to obtain a proper fit in the first place. Likewise the wrist of the rifle, where the trigger hand grips it, can vary. If you have small hands, you do not want to strain to grip the rifle firmly, or to reach the trigger. Any competent gunsmith will be able to advise you if a rifle is right for you. If it is not, try another.

Finally, before purchasing your rifle you will need to apply to the police for a Firearms Certificate (FAC). Before you apply, you need a good idea of not only what calibre you want that rifle to be in, but what it is to be used for and where it is to be used, as the final certificate issued to you will be very conditional. If, for example, it does not specify use for vermin control, you will fall foul of the law if you start shooting foxes. You will also be required to provide proof of the landowner's permission to use the rifle on his ground. Experienced stalkers can be very helpful when it comes to completing the FAC application paperwork, as can the police firearms department for your area, and of course you will get invaluable advice if you attend a DSC1 course.

Telescopic Sights

It is, of course, possible to shoot with open (iron) sights and not bother with expensive telescopic sights. But look at the advantages of the latter. More precise

A selection of telescopic sights, ranging from a fixed-power 6x42 (top) through a number of variable-power models. Be wary of excessive magnification which is more suited to long range vermin shooting. In addition, the large object lenses on some models can demand high mounts if they are to be kept clear of the rifle barrel. If in doubt, the best bet is to keep it simple while buying the best quality that you can afford.

aiming, especially at longer ranges, and an ability to pick out the details of your target when the natural light available makes use of the naked eye impossible are but two. As many of your chances are likely to come at dawn or dusk, or in the gloom of a thick wood, the last reason is perhaps the most overwhelming argument in favour. Don't be misled by those who claim that telescopic sights are unsporting. We are looking for an accurate, humane shot, and anything that tilts the balance in our direction is well worth using. It's no accident that fewer and fewer sporting rifles are leaving the factory with iron sights fitted.

You are going to ask a lot of your telescopic sight. After all, it is a delicate optical instrument that is expected to absorb day-to-day handling, travelling to and from your stalking grounds, and on top of this cope with the heavy recoil of a full-bore rifle. And all this while retaining the ability to put shot after shot into the same place without losing its zero.

It follows that it is worth spending your money on a quality model. There are plenty of cheap 'scopes on the market, but beware the lightweight models designed for air rifles or .22s. These will simply not stand up to the hammering recoil of a full bore. At the lower price ranges, you can find some good working tools which are made largely in Japan. But the Continental manufacturers, such as Zeiss or Swarovski, remain the cream of the crop. Apart from their general robustness and tendency to come with a long guarantee, just comparing the clarity of one with an inexpensive counterpart should be enough to convince. The accepted wisdom in most quarters is that you don't need to spend too much on the rifle, but every penny that you can afford on the 'scope.

What magnification? The choice can be bewildering, with fixed or variable-power lenses of all kinds available. By all means go for the latter but take care with the budget end of the market. With a cheap 'scope the point of zero for the rifle can shift as the magnification of the 'scope is increased or decreased. You also need to take care that the 'scope clears the barrel of the rifle when fitted – some have very large bells at the object lens end and may not sit high enough to clear the barrel. A fixed power 'scope is much more straightforward.

I favour 6x magnification, but agree with the opinion of many woodland stalkers that 4x can be better at close ranges where you are looking to bring the rifle to bear on the target quickly.

Telescopic sights are usually described using two numbers – 4 x 32, 6 x 42, 4-10 x 52 and so on. The first number indicates the magnification (or the range of magnification as in the last example). The second is the diameter of the object lens in millimetres. Put simply, the combination of the two determines the light-gathering capability of the 'scope (see the section on binoculars below). Any model designed for stalking today should perform well in low light but take care with variable power models. As you increase the magnification, insufficient light is gathered by the object lens and the quality of the sight picture diminishes. 6 x 42 and 4 x 32 are both a widely available 'scope patterns, and are generally considered to be good working combinations for most stalking conditions.

Of great importance is the graticule pattern. This is what you see when you aim the rifle, and once again there can seem to be almost too much choice. What you are looking for is a combination that allows you to take a fine aim in as many light conditions as possible. Thin cross hairs tend to disappear as the light goes, but thick ones are not sufficient for precise aim. Some manufacturers even offer cross hairs, or red dots, that can be illuminated by a battery built in to the 'scope body. Of all the sighting arrangements available, for my money the best is the 'Duplex' - four thick posts converging on to finer crosshairs. These allow for a good sight picture to be obtained in all conditions. With practice, you also get the added advantage of being able to confirm the range to your target by knowing how a deer fits between the posts of the sight (although this should be used as no more than a last-moment check to confirm the range immediately before you take the shot – a telescopic sight must never be used in place of binoculars).

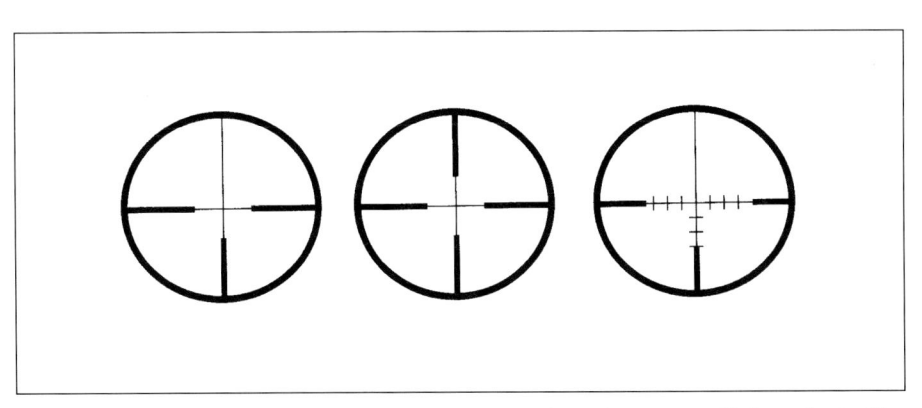

A range of graticule patterns suitable for woodland stalking

View through telescopic sight, showing the graticule pattern.

'Swing off' mounts permit the sight to be removed from the rifle quickly and easily.

Don't forget the mounts, the means by which the telescopic sight is secured to the rifle. Make sure that the correct ones for the model of rifle are fitted – and that they match the 'scope. Sight tubes can come in three diameters; 30mm, the Continental 26mm, or one inch. Trying to secure a metric 'scope to an Imperial set of mounts can be disastrous! Going to a competent rifle smith will ensure that all is fitted properly. It is possible to get 'swing-off' mounts, which allow the sight to be removed from the rifle and be refitted without any loss of zero, but again seek advice first and beware of the cheaper models. In my book the only real advantage of swing-off mounts is the ability to switch to iron sights (if fitted) should the 'scope become unserviceable (say, after a knock) and an animal has to be followed up. Personally, I prefer my sight to be a permanent part of the rifle – less to go wrong, resulting in greater confidence in the overall system.

Finally, you need to protect the lenses of the sight in wet weather. There is nothing more irritating to find, as you come to take a shot, that they are covered in rain and impossible to see through. Most 'scopes come with lens covers joined by elastic or rubber to hold them in place. Some are transparent, but don't try to look through them to shoot as they are not intended for this purpose and lack clarity. By attaching the elastic straps to the 'scope body with rubber bands or electrical tape, you will ensure that you don't lose them. Better yet, invest in a pair of flip-up lens covers which are much better, and pop up out of the way at the touch of a button.

Sound Moderators
You would be sensible to consider the fitting of a sound moderator (often referred to as a suppressor or a silencer) to your rifle. The moderator works by

By securing the elastic that joins the covers to the sight itself with electricians tape, you will ensure that they are not lost when removed.

Flip-up lens covers are a very convenient option.

venting the gases, caused by the explosion that drives the bullet, through a series of baffles. These baffles lower the pressure at which the gases vent into the atmosphere by cooling and condensing them, and so reduce the noise of that venting. A moderator will not completely remove the sound of a stalking rifle being fired, but it can reduce it to the point that it sounds rather like a standard round from a .22 rimfire rifle. With high velocity ammunition, of course, the supersonic 'crack' of the bullet in flight cannot be suppressed.

True, a moderator adds overall length and weight to the set-up, but consider the advantages. Firstly, disturbance to the environment is vastly reduced. This increases your chances of getting shot at another animal later in the outing; it also means that those living within a mile or so of your stalking grounds are less likely to be disturbed at unsociable hours. Users of moderators can also quickly realise that their shooting accuracy is much improved as recoil can be reduced by up to one third. The slight weight increase is not really an issue, as we are not talking about carrying the rifle all day over long distances, as we would if stalking, say, red deer in the Highlands.

Sound moderators do not have to add excessive length to a rifle, as modern designs can sleeve back over the barrel. This Steyr Scout is compact and has an integral bipod.

Very importantly, your hearing will be subject to less damage. Hopefully we all wear ear defenders on the rifle range, but how many people stop to put them on once into the stalk? It's easy to say that the occasional round won't hurt, but consider the cumulative effect over the years. Take it from one who knows!

You must have provision on your Firearms Certificate to allow the use of a sound moderator. However, most police forces are becoming increasingly enlightened in this respect, mainly on environmental and hearing protection grounds. If you do decide to follow this route, bear in mind that the moderator must be fitted by a rifle smith (it's a relatively simple, if skilled, procedure to cut a thread at the muzzle end of the barrel) and then subjected to proof testing. Don't be tempted to do it yourself, no matter how good you are with a lathe.

Other Rifle Fittings

Unlike the highland stalker who tends to keep his rifle in a slip until the very final approach of the stalk, the woodland stalker needs to have his rifle constantly ready for immediate use, so a good rifle sling is essential. Make sure that it has a non-slip backing and it is not excessively wide, or you will be constantly adjusting it on the shoulder. As your rifle will spend most of its time in this position it's worth ensuring that you will be comfortable and, importantly, not making unnecessary movements that may alert your quarry. Braided leather designs are excellent, as is rubber-backed canvas, but whatever you choose be careful of the means by which the sling is attached to the rifle. Heavy buckles

The sling should hold the rifle comfortably on the shoulder and have no fittings that will knock against or damage the woodwork.

Bipods require a somewhat different technique, and practice on the range is essential before use for shooting at a live target

or studs can knock against the rifle, making noise and scratching the woodwork. Leather thronging is a much better option.

Bipods are becoming increasingly popular, and are a considerable aid to accuracy when on the rifle range or when stalking open ground. I would question the practicality of one for woodland stalking, however. In return for adding extra weight to the rifle you gain few advantages. The opportunities for prone shots in typical muntjac habitat are very few and far between, and you will waste precious time unfolding the bipod legs and setting yourself up for a shot on the rare occasions that they do.

By all means invest in a bipod if you think that you will have opportunities to use it, but make sure that it is easily detachable from the rifle for those stalking expeditions where there is simply no need. Bipods come in a variety of heights, and those designed for sitting or kneeling shooting are especially useful if you spend a lot of time waiting in ambush from a vantage point. Go for a model with a swivelling rather than a fixed head, and get used to using it on the range. Bipods can take a little getting used to, and may well alter the point of zero for your rifle.

Binoculars
Over the years I have used a variety of binoculars for stalking – Second World War vintage, modern Army issue and more recently a brand name Japanese model in the 'affordable' price range. By and large, all were acceptable in their own way and I was quite satisfied with them. I was spotting deer well enough and, I thought, studying them in reasonable detail.

Then I splashed out on an expensive (and I mean expensive) pair of Austrian-made binoculars and my life changed. The difference in quality was a revelation. I was not only seeing into cover, but through it. Deer leapt into stunning detail when before they would have been indistinct. Dawn and dusk were extended considerably as I sat in a high seat, able to observe around me for so much longer. It didn't take me long to realise that my stalking had been marred for years by my own stinginess.

What you decide upon depends invariably on your budget. It is easy to spend many hundreds of pounds on top-of-the-range binoculars, but in truth you can, with care, find something perfectly serviceable for much less. Your needs are simple. Your binoculars must be light, easy to focus, and of sufficient quality for you to examine a deer in close detail at 100 metres, or detect it's presence at up to 500 metres. They must work well in poor light conditions, be steady in use, and well enough constructed not to let in the damp and fog up. If you wear spectacles, the eye pieces must be able to fold or roll down so that you can use them together.

Most stalkers find that 7x or 8x magnification is about right. Go higher and you'll find them too heavy to hold steady, effectively cancelling out any advantage in higher magnifications. Like telescopic sights, binoculars are described using two figures, for example 7 x 50 or 8 x 30. The first figure is the magnification, the second the size of the object lens. The relationship between the two is actually quite important. If you divide the diameter of the object lens by the magnification, you arrive at a figure known as the exit pupil. Thus the exit pupil of a pair of 7 x 50 binoculars is about 7mm, and that of a pair of 8 x 30 is only $3^{3}/_{4}$mm. As the maximum aperture of the human eye is itself 7mm, this is the optimum exit pupil for a pair of binoculars. Any higher number is simply wasted - the eye cannot adjust far enough to take advantage of it. The same principle applies to telescopic sights.

Having said that, developments in modern optics are such that, the more you pay, the better the quality of equipment that you end up with. My Austrian 7 x 42s, despite having a smaller exit pupil, are hugely superior to the bargain-basement 7 x 50s – whilst being smaller, lighter and having a wider field of view. You get what you pay for. So the best advice I can offer is to spend as much as you can afford. You won't regret it. Whatever your budget, you can do a lot worse than go to a specialist supplier of optical equipment who will be able to give you proper guidance on the choices available. These can often be found at Game Fairs and other country shows, which themselves offer a good opportunity to 'try before you buy'.

Some binoculars, especially the cheaper ones, come with thin nylon straps which are murderously uncomfortable on the neck after a couple of hours in the woods. Invest in a neoprene strap which spreads the weight and you'll hardly notice them. Better still, you can now buy harnesses that loop over your shoulders and redistribute the weight even more, holding the binoculars snug against your chest. They are especially good when crawling – no need to take the binos off or tuck them inside your jacket to stop them dragging on the ground.

A variety of binoculars. The old 7x50s on the left are good but heavy and not particularly water-resistant; they fog up easily in the damp. The modern budget-price 7x50s in the centre are better and rubber-armoured, although they offer a narrow field of view and the optical quality is relatively low. However, the 7x42s on the right are of superb quality and, despite a smaller exit pupil than the 7x50s, produce exceptional clarity even in poor light. All have lens covers, either home made or as supplied by the manufacturer, to prevent rain getting onto the lens.

As with your telescopic sight, the lenses need protecting in wet weather. You can use the covers which come with the binoculars when you first buy them (making sure that they are secured to the neck strap so that they don't get lost the first time you take them off in the field), but if this is impractical or they are awkward to use, there is a cheap, easy and effective alternative. Simply thread a leather flap onto the neck strap so that it hangs over the binocular lenses when they are not in use, and falls out of the way when you lift them.

Sticks

There are still people who never carry a stick when stalking. Don't be the same and deny yourself the advantages of carrying one. A good hazel stick is a simple thing, strong enough to support your weight without bending when leant on, and about the same height as yourself. It will steady your rifle when shooting from the standing position – something that the woodland stalker tends to do a lot of. It will also give you invaluable support crossing rough ground or climbing a steer hill, or probe ditches and muddy patches before you commit yourself to crossing. You'll soon get used to carrying it, and feel naked without it after a while.

Better yet, use a double stick. A suitable pole can be split lengthways and joined with a bolt or similar fixing. Easier yet, a visit to the garden centre will find you two 6' plastic-covered garden poles (the sort used as an alternative to bamboo canes). These can be hinged at the top by a lashing of bicycle inner tube, a rubber drive loop stolen from the family vacuum cleaner, or a bridle fitting bought from the saddlers. The double stick gives you much more stability. When a single stick will move from side to side when the rifle is in the aim,

Double sticks in use - a very steady way to shoot from a standing position

Two plastic garden canes joined by rubber bridle fittings. The smaller diameter rings can be slipped onto individual sticks to prevent them from clattering together. The top of each cane has been bound with electricians tape to prevent scratching the rifles woodwork.

the double forms a tripod with your body and provides for very steady shooting indeed. A simple set-up like this will cost you just a few pounds. If you are willing to part with more cash, you can buy very swish telescopic double sticks, made of aluminium and very strong, from stalking goods suppliers.

Some people go to extremes and construct tripods of three poles joined together – very steady but awkward to bring into use smoothly. I have also seen Continental 'mountain sticks' for sale in this country, lightweight and cunningly joined four-piece poles that look like two inverted 'Vs. These provide an unbelievably solid rifle support – so much so that you could zero a weapon from them – but sadly you almost need a graduate degree to use them. My advice is to keep things simple –after all, by the time you have brought the rifle to bear, you don't want your intended target to have long since moved on.

Clothing

Your clothing requirements for stalking are simple. Anything that is quiet, comfortable and unobtrusive as you go about the woods is suitable. Sadly, waxed or oiled jackets, very popular for other shooting sports do not fit the bill, as they tend to be noisy in use. The invention of Gore-tex and other semi-permeable membrane linings has spawned a profusion of suitable clothing from which you can make your choice. Many are purpose-made for stalking and very good indeed.

Camouflage patterns have become incredibly realistic and are deservedly popular, but do not discount military surplus which can be very cheap and serviceable. If you spend more money, you do of course end up with 'all seasons' clothing with zip-out fleeces and waterproof liners. By adopting a layering principle your stalking clothes can adapt between sweltering hot summer evenings and sub-zero winter mornings.

I have found that camouflage, whilst having its place, can be a disadvantage as well. When the leaves are off the trees in winter it can actually make you stand out, and at such times I prefer to wear a plain, mossy-green coat. Another problem with camouflage is that you can end up looking disconcertingly like Rambo and potentially alarming to anyone you might meet in the woods. Whatever you choose to wear, make sure that you avoid washing powders with brightening or bleaching agents to clean it. Otherwise you will reflect ultra violet light and be more visible to the deer.

The stalker has a vast array of suitable clothing to choose from on the modern market. Camouflage is not essential; what is important is that the garment is quiet in use, unobtrusive and comfortable.

Footwear is a personal choice. You need to be able to feel the ground beneath the foot to ensure that you move quietly, so heavy boots are out. In summer, lightweight plimsolls or moccasins are great as long as you don't mind wet feet from dew-laden undergrowth. The key to good stalking footwear is a sensitive sole; a good compromise is a well-fitting pair of Wellington boots or a combination of light boots and gaiters. These will not only keep your feet dry, and thus warm and comfortable, but also stop ticks and the like from getting access to your bare skin. Although I have seen camouflage pattern boots on the market, this is a bit extreme and colour is not really an issue – if the deer can see your feet they will probably have seen other parts of you first.

Hats are a very personal choice. It's a good job that woodland stalking is a largely solitary sport as there are some extraordinary creations to be seen out there! There is no problem in indulging yourself as long as your hat is unobtrusive in the same way as the rest of your clothing. It should have a brim that will not only shade your eyes from the sun and rain, but also help to conceal your face from the deer.

A snug-fitting, lightweight pair of gloves that you can wear when shooting are a must. In colder weather they can be worn in conjunction with palmless mittens. When you are lining up for a shot it is no time to be taking your gloves off. Your hands will be constantly up and down with binoculars as you observe about you, and the movement of white hands will be quickly picked up by your quarry. For the same reason, a mask of the sort used by pigeon shooters is a great help and conceals your face – another patch of unnatural paleness as far as the deer are concerned. When I was younger and keener, I used to use military camouflage cream. Net veils are an easier option; you are also more likely to remember to take them off when you stop at the pub on the way home!

Knives

You see some extraordinary knives carried by stalkers – big, heavy things with Bowie blades that look more suitable for wrestling crocodiles than basic gralloching and skinning work. The truth of the matter is that you don't need a big blade. Three inches of steel is more than adequate. The trick it to keep it for deer and not to use it for day-to-day tasks that will blunt, or worse still, damage the blade. One good knife will serve all of your stalking needs, but specialist skinning, boning or filleting knives all have their uses once in the larder.

What you are looking for is pretty simple. A non-slip handle, with a guard to stop the hand slipping down onto the blade when slick with blood, and a blade that will take a good edge – and hold it. Cheap stainless steel is difficult to get a good working edge on. The whole thing needs to be easily cleaned to ensure that blood, hair and other debris is totally removed. For this reason I would recommend going for a fixed-blade knife rather than one that folds. You can get handles made of some very exotic materials, but plastic or rubber win hands down for ease of cleaning. Simply put them in the dishwasher, or soak and scrub in the

A selection of practical stalking knives, with a 6" ruler for comparison. Top: plastic handle and sheath, with the added advantage of a brightly coloured handle – a very practical knife that can be washed along with its sheath in a dishwasher. Centre: wooden handle and leather sheath. Bottom: antler handled skinning knife – a thinner blade which sharpens to a very keen edge but is not robust enough for heavier cutting.

sink. Brightly coloured handles are also a good idea. They may not be as attractive as natural materials, but are much easier to find after you put them down in long grass when dealing with an animal in the half light of dawn or dusk.

You can spend a lot of money on a good knife. By all means do so, but there is no need to go mad. For as little as ten pounds you can pick up something that meets all your needs – and not lose sleep if you leave it in the middle of nowhere in all the excitement of getting your freshly-shot animal home.

Give a thought to the sheath as well. It should be solid enough to ensure that the blade cannot come through if, say, you were to fall awkwardly on it. Like the knife, it needs to be easily cleaned. How many people religiously clean their knife – then put it back into a leather sheath, the inside of which is caked with blood from previous outings? A plastic sheath may not be as pretty as the hand-tooled leather article, but once again it can be popped into the dishwasher after use.

Above all keep your knife sharp. Blunt blades cut more people; the less effort you have to put into cutting, the less chance there is of an accident. Not all of us are blessed with the ability to use a sharpening steel, but there are some excellent idiot-proof sharpening systems on the market that ensure that the blade is held at a constant angle as the stone moves over it. These are first-class investments which will pay for themselves over and over again. You'll be popular at home too, as the cook's tools take on a new lease of life!

Other Accessories
Once you have actually shot your deer, you will need some means of extracting it from the woods. Forget dragging, if only to protect the carcase from contamination. You will need to get it off the ground while making it easily transportable. At least here the muntjac stalker has a huge advantage over his

A simple strap of leather measuring about 65 x 6 cm, with a loop at each corner, can be slipped into a pocket and makes easy work of shouldering out a carcase.

Carrying strap in use. A small piece of waterproof material covering the wound area will protect your clothes from blood.

A purpose-made stalkers rucksack. This one has an easily-washed detachable lining and convenient pockets. It is made of a Loden material that is very quiet in use.

counterpart who has to shift a red stag off the Highland hill! You have a number of options available. You can tie the legs together and sling it over your shoulder, or use your stick for the same purpose. Both become uncomfortable very quickly. A simple strap of leather, similar in width to a luggage shoulder strap and equipped with loops that fit over the knee joints of the animal, allows it to be simply shouldered and carried out.

Alternately, a rucksack is much more comfortable and can also be used to carry spare clothing, items of equipment and even your packed lunch. A trip to a military surplus store will find you something practical. Alternately, a purpose-made roe sack is even better and a standard one will accommodate a big muntjac buck or two smaller deer. These come with removable waterproof linings which prevent blood getting onto your clothing and can be scrubbed out once home, making the sack a much more hygienic option. Made of canvas or a similar light but strong material, choosing one with a couple of external pockets means that you can store other items and not overload your pockets.

In addition, you should consider carrying the following items of equipment:

Spare ammunition – never shoot at a deer with your last round. You never know what opportunities are going to present themselves, and not having the means to finish off a wounded animal humanely is inexcusable. A small pouch with loops or compartments will stop rounds from rattling in your pocket.

Torch – head lamps leave both hands free and are very useful for performing a gralloch at dusk, or packing a heavy load out of the woods in the dark. A spare set of batteries can save frustration.

First Aid Kit – if you carry one the chances are that you won't need it, but if you do you can bet that it will be in a hurry. Nothing too comprehensive is needed, just a small selection of bandages and sticking plasters. Small kits the size of tobacco tins can be obtained from any camping supplier.

Rifle cleaning kit – for removing blockages from the rifle barrel and other emergency cleaning. A collapsible rod, brush and jag with some oil and flannelette might mean all the difference between making your rifle safe and serviceable in the field or having to go home to do the job.

Bolt sheath – you should never transport a rifle with the bolt in place in case the unthinkable happens and it is stolen. A bolt sheath loops onto your belt and is a safe place to store it when it is removed. It is equally useful as its presence reminds you to actually take the bolt with you when you go stalking – you'd be surprised how easy it is to forget, especially when you are in a rush or during a bleary early-morning start.

Spare knife – in case you forget or lose yours, or it loses its edge.

Whistle and small strobe light – for emergency signalling. The strobe light is also useful for mark a carcase position at night if you have to leave it and return later, or to attach to your dog's collar if conducting a follow-up in the dark.

Compass and map – you'd be surprised how easy it is to get lost, even on fairly familiar ground, and especially at night. A small orienteering compass weighs next to nothing and points you in the right direction.

Folding shovel – for burying grallochs.

Mobile telephone – very useful in emergencies, or for simply warning your household that you will be late home. Make sure that you have numbers such as the estate office, gamekeeper and local police programmed into the address book in case you need them in a hurry. Walkie-talkie radios are also very useful if two or more people are stalking the same ground. They are relatively inexpensive and have a range of up to two miles, although in woodland this can be much reduced. Go for a model with an earpiece and collar microphone option, making it silent in use.

Notebook and pencil – for recording anything unusual, from suspicious vehicle details to wildlife observations. A small 'single use' camera is also very handy.

Tissue paper – in addition to the obvious use, very useful for marking blood splashes, otherwise difficult to see, when following up a wounded animal, cleaning binocular or sight lenses, etc. Aways keep a few sheets in a plastic sleeve with your notebook.

Latex or rubber gloves and plastic bags – for performing the gralloch (no need to go hunting for water to wash your hands afterwards) and carrying liver and kidneys etc.

Light nylon line or 'para cord' - hundreds of uses, from an emergency rifle sling to carrying a carcase or simply replacing a broken bootlace.

Electrical or masking tape – apart from all kinds of emergency repair jobs, a small strip of tape across the muzzle of the rifle stops rain, mud and other debris getting into the barrel. This has no effect on accuracy, as the pressure generated by the firing of the bullet blows it out of the way long before the bullet reaches the muzzle.

Firearms Certificate and letter of permission – a policeman has the right to confiscate your rifle if you cannot produce your FAC. Likewise, a letter of

A basic stalking kit. In addition to rifle, jacket, hat and stalking sticks, it contains the following (clockwise from top left): disposable gloves, plastic bags & electricians tape; firearm certificate, notebook & pencil (in plastic bag); tissues; spare ammunition; binoculars; knife; call; rifle bolt (in belt sheath); face mask & gloves.

Rucksack contents (clockwise from top left): spare knife; head lamp; first aid kit; compass; rifle cleaning kit; whistle; strobe light; nylon line.

permission to stalk from the landowner is useful if you are challenged. Neither of them is any use sitting in the desk at home when you need them. Sealing them in a plastic bag means that they can live in an inside jacket pocket without being spoilt by damp or dirt.

This list is by no means exhaustive, and you will find that the stalking market offers any number of supposedly invaluable gadgets. Take care, as it's easy to overload yourself. A friend of mine does an annual clearout of all the 'useful' items that he has accumulated in his roe sack and stalking jacket. It's amazing how many he never uses. Experience will show you what you actually need – in reality, as long as you have a rifle, ammunition, binoculars and knife, you have the basic equipment to stalk. As for the rest – the needs of a stalker will vary according to the size, location and terrain of their ground. Whatever else you carry is very much up to you and your own particular circumstances.

Some useful items kept in the car: a plastic storage box (this one will take two muntjac easily and the lid keeps the contents from prying eyes); a folding shovel for burying grallochs; a folding saw for cutting branches that obscure high seat fields of vision; a multi-tool for any number of purposes.

11/2/2019

A unicorn

by

Stella

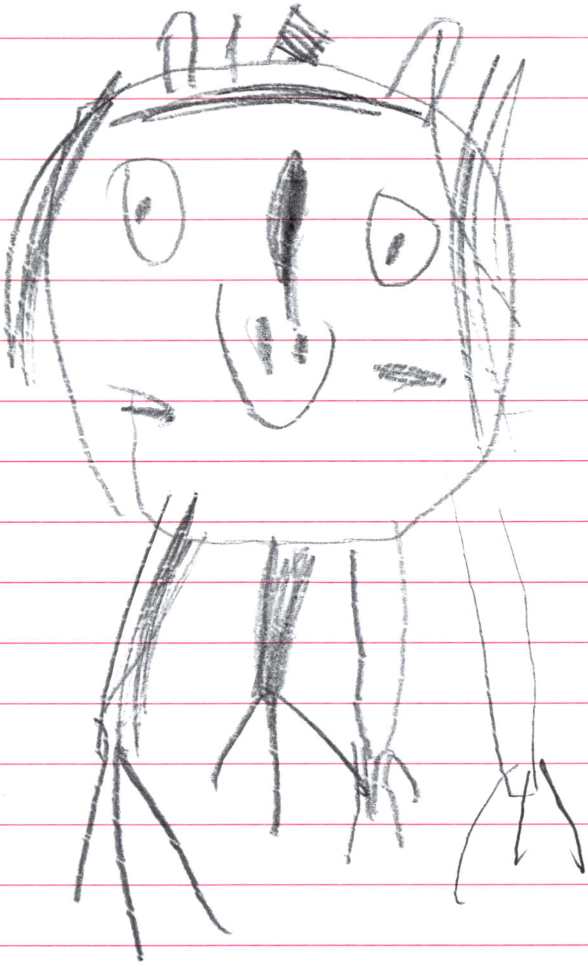

CHAPTER 5
Range Work

You will probably have spent a considerable amount of money on your rifle, scope and other equipment. The trick now is to ensure that you use them to the best advantage. Modern rifles, even mass-produced models, are capable of quite astonishing levels of accuracy if set up and used properly, and it is easily possible for a total newcomer to full-bore rifle shooting to achieve this in a short period of time with a little practice.

Consider yourself and your rifle to be part of a sophisticated weapons system; if all the elements of that system are in harmony you will achieve the results that you are looking for. If not, frustration is the most likely outcome. It is therefore worth spending a bit of time pulling things together. Let's not forget, either, that our ultimate target is not a piece of cardboard but a living, breathing animal that we want to kill cleanly with a single, well-aimed shot. Muntjac are perhaps the most demanding of the British deer in this respect as they are relatively small and do not stay still for long. Before shooting at one, the conscientious stalker will want to build up the confidence that comes with total familiarity with his rifle.

Muntjac are a relatively small and very mobile target; it follows that shooting skills need the be of the highest possible standard if the stalker is to be successful as well as humane

Setting Up

If you have bought a second-hand rifle, the chances are that it will have come with the telescopic sight already mounted. If not, or if it is new, the job will need to be done properly to ensure that the ensemble is properly and solidly put together. This is not difficult in itself, although if you are buying from a gunsmith he will be able to do it for you.

The scope mounts are a very important part of the overall system, and it is surprising how many people pay a great deal of money on a rifle and scope, then skimp on the key element that connects them. Buy good ones - they will repay you in reliability and through it increased confidence. Cheap mounts can be worse than useless. Some people swear by swing-off mounts; I must confess that my one of my rifles is fitted with very high quality set, but after years of use I still lack complete confidence in them and don't use them. In any case most modern rifles come without iron sights fitted anyway. I suggest that you go for good quality, standard mounts. Get a competent gunsmith to fit them. It can be done at home but is best left to an expert if anything but the most simple fitting is needed.

It is important that the scope is fixed with the sighting graticules level on the rifle, otherwise you will cant it while aiming and affect accuracy. This can be done in the garden, with the help of a spirit level and a 'workmate' vice or something similar to hold the rifle firmly. Set up a sheet of paper with a horizontal line on it some twenty to thirty metres away, using the spirit level to ensure that the line is truly horizontal. A piece of string between two bamboo stakes is just as effective. Then lay the rifle in the vice and place the level across one set of the scope mounts (with the top half removed). When horizontal, clamp the rifle firmly (don't forget to use rags to protect the woodwork if necessary). Now, lay the scope on top of the lower mounts and fix the upper halves of the mounts loosely in place.

Use a spirit level to ensure that both rifle and the horizontal sighting line are truly level before mounting the scope

Having ensured that the rifle and sighting line are both perfectly level, the scope can be rotated in the mounts until the graticule and the sighting line are parallel.

At this point ensure that you are allowing sufficient distance between the scope and your eye when shooting from prone; most scopes are set up for an eye relief of about one inch. Allow too little eye relief and you'll find that the scope recoils onto your eyebrow when you fire the rifle, a potential cause of flinching. It helps to experiment before you start the scope mounting process, making a light pencil mark on the scope tube that will show you the right positioning when you move on to the next step.

Now it is simply a matter of aligning the horizontal line on the sheet of paper with the one that you can see through the scope. You'll find that it is easier to move the paper than the rifle and clamp, which will otherwise have to be constantly relevelled. Once you can see the paper through the scope, roll the sight in its mounts until the graticule and the horizontal line are parallel. Once this is done to your satisfaction, simply tighten the fixing screws on the mounts to secure the scope. Don't screw each one down tight in one go - move around them doing the job gradually. A dab of Tippex or coloured paint at the point where scope and mount meet completes the job. This will show you instantly at any time in the future if the scope has moved.

A dab of paint where the mounts meet the scope tube will provide a visual warning if anything has moved out of place

Ammunition

A brief word on ammunition might be appropriate at this point. Any modern factory loaded ammunition of the correct calibre will shoot accurately through a modern rifle, but you will find that some are better than others when matched with your rifle. This is down to a combination of the powder loads used, bullet size and shape, headspacing and any number of other factors that combine when the bullet is fired. The differences between various cartridge loads and the rifles they are used in may be tiny, but they are capable of having a big effect on accuracy. Sometimes the variations in accuracy can mean an inch or two at a hundred metres.

As a rule of thumb – an a very general one at that – I have found that American ammunition (such as Winchester or Federal) tends to work well with American built rifles, while European ammunition (Norma, RWS, Sako etc) suits European rifles. I am aware that I am making a very dangerous statement here, as there are always exceptions to the rule! Certainly my Brno .308 (a Czech manufacturer) performs very well with Winchester ammunition. Try various brands. You will find, with experimentation, one that produces the best results in your rifle.

Bullet design is important. Not only must the bullet expand on hitting the target to ensure maximum effect, but the copper skin must be strong enough to stop it doing so, or breaking up, too early. It is especially important if you are using one of the smaller calibres, such as the .243, that you use bullets designed for use on deer. The lighter 'varminting' bullets intended for foxes and small vermin are too light for our purposes and could easily cause superficial surface wounds that do not kill cleanly.

If you reload your own ammunition you will be able to work up loads that not only produce optimum results but also make your shooting practice much cheaper. Reloading is a fascinating subject in its own right, but needs to be taught to you by an expert if the results are to be safe. Regular courses are run by the BDS and shooting organisations such as the BASC; these are a good alternative to on-to-one tuition by an experienced friend.

Buy your ammunition in batches – I suggest at least a hundred rounds at a time – and check that the batch number on each box is the same. Although it may seem expensive all in one go, it is no more so than buying several lots of boxes of twenty. You will always have a reserve available for practice and stalking, and more importantly you will not need to check zero so frequently.

It makes good sense to buy your ammunition in batches of at least 100 rounds. The hand-written letter on the side of the box identifies a particular batch and prevents any accidental mixing of different ones.

Manufacturers may change load specifications without warning, and you should never fire a round from a new batch at a living deer without first checking the point of zero.

Collimators and Bore Sighting
Before you actually fire a shot from the rifle you will want to be sure that it will land somewhere on the target before you can go onto the fine-tuning process of zeroing. If a gunsmith has set the rifle up for you, he will probably have used a collimator to do this. Also known as a scope sighter, shot saver or similar trade name, a collimator is a device that is fixed onto the end of the rifle barrel using a rod appropriate to the rifle calibre. When you look through the scope, it shows you a grid of horizontal and vertical lines (rather like graph paper). By adjusting the scope reticules so that they centre on the grid, you can be sure that the first zeroing shot from the rifle will be close to the aiming point on the target.

Collimator fitted to the rifle using a rod appropriate to the calibre and plugged into the barrel

Collimator grid as seen through the telescopic sight

The value of a collimator does not diminish once a rifle has been zeroed. By keeping a record of where the graticule lies against the grid when the rifle is 'on', the collimator can be fitted at any time in the future to check quickly that it has not shifted for any reason - say, after a long journey, a suspect shot or if you suspect that the scope has taken a knock. This will not only save you the time and expense of check zeroing before every outing, but also greatly boost your confidence in your rifle and scope. As such, it is well worth considering investing in a collimator.

If you do not have access to a collimator, though, it is not the end of the world. It is a simple matter to bore sight your rifle. Simply clamp it loosely and place a target a short distance away (again, the far end of the garden is fine).

With the bolt removed, look through the barrel from the stock end and line the rifle up with the target. Now adjust the scope graticules so that they too are aligned with the target and the rifle is bore sighted. The first shot is very unlikely to be dead centre, but it will be close enough to allow proper zeroing to commence.

Basic Shooting Technique

Before you fire your first shot, take a few moments to prepare the rifle. Check that all of the bedding screws are tight and ensure that there are no traces of oil in the barrel. The smallest amount of oil can cause a bullet to fly wild, and a large amount can be positively dangerous. Keep running flannelette patches through the barrel with a cleaning rod and jag until they come out clean.

If you are new to full bore rifle shooting, concentrate on getting your technique right before attempting to zero your weapon. Old soldiers, used to the kick of a rifle, generally have little to learn, but newcomers may find the prospect daunting. It isn't. A rifle kicks no more really than a 12 bore shotgun, but whereas the shotgun is an 'area weapon' the rifle is a precision tool designed to deliver a single projectile with considerable accuracy. Start at a range of about 25 or 30 metres from the target - if the sights are slightly out, your shots will be more likely to be somewhere on the target anyway (three inches from centre at 25 metres is a foot at 100 metres). Don't try anything fancy to begin with; do your shooting from a prone position and use a sandbag or something similar as a support. It is always useful to remember that you will not feel the kick of the rifle until the bullet has long since left the barrel and is on it's way to the target.

Don't forget to wear ear defenders!

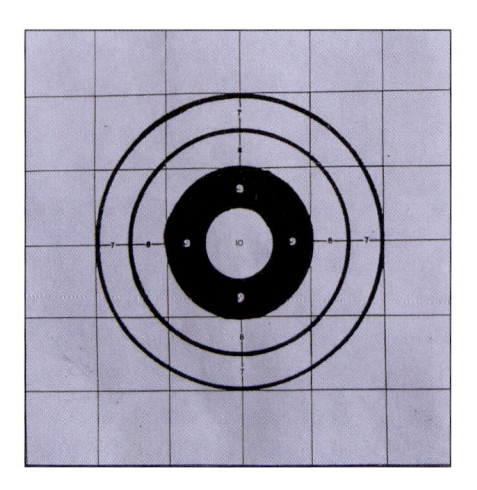

A suitable target for both basic practice and zeroing – this sort is used in the first part of the DSC Level 1 shooting test. Each square represents one inch.

Get comfortable behind the rifle. If you are right handed, it is this hand that grips the rifle and pulls it firmly into your shoulder. The left hand is simply a support; rest it on a sandbag to keep it steady. Relax, and concentrate on your breathing. As you exhale the sights should drift naturally onto the target - if they don't, adjust your position until they do. After a deep breath, simply exhale, ensure that you are on target and gently squeeze (don't jerk) the trigger. Don't hold yourself in the aim for too long, or you will find that you start to shake. Try to get into the habit of aiming, exhaling and squeezing the trigger in a set routine. Some rifles come with 'two stage' triggers, which have a degree of slack to take up before firing, others have none at all. Most are adjustable; although you do not want the trigger pressure to be too light, neither should it require too heavy a pull. A gunsmith will be able to make adjustments to suit you. It pays to familiarise yourself with your rifle before you move to live firing, but even so it should almost come as a surprise when the rifle goes off.

A comfortable firing position is important. Here the firer is using a stalking sack. Sandbags, where available, are excellent supports.

A good coach will watch the firer, not the target, and be able to advise a shooter on his technique

Fire a few more rounds, a total of three is usually enough, taking the same point of aim and keeping your breathing the same. If all has gone well the bullet holes will lie in a tight group on the target. No worry if they are not in the centre as you haven't zeroed the rifle yet. You are looking for no more than putting your shots into the same place, hopefully in a group of an inch or less at this stage. You'll find that practice reduces the group size still further. Once you are grouping well you can adjust the sights if necessary to ensure that your shots are falling into the centre of the target, and consider moving back to a longer range to zero the rifle properly.

It will help if you have an experienced shot with you to act as a coach. He will be watching you, not the target, when you fire to make sure that your technique is correct. Quite often a good coach will pick up problems that the shooter is not even aware of and can save you a great deal of trouble in the long run. Particular things to look out for include flinching as a result of anticipating the sound and kick of the rifle, snatching at the trigger rather than squeezing, and incorrect breathing. A good coach will be able to guide, reassure and encourage a firer at the same time, identifying faults and improving his subject's shooting skills rapidly.

Don't keep on shooting until the rifle barrel is red hot. Rest yourself between groups of shots. An overheated barrel will reduce accuracy - never forget that in stalking it is the first shot from a cold barrel that is important.

Zeroing

If you are an experienced shot you may have skipped the basic practice and moved straight to the zeroing stage. Having bore sighted the rifle, fire a single shot at the point of aim (POA) at a fairly close range - say, 25 or 30 metres. Then secure the rifle with the cross hairs of the sight fixed on the POA. Adjust the cross hairs until they lie on the bullet hole in the target, fire a second shot to confirm the adjustment, and you are ready to move back to a longer range to complete the zeroing process.

Opinions vary on ideal zeroing ranges but it is generally agreed that 100 metres is about right (convenient, as this tends to be the distance between firing point and target on most formal rifle ranges). A group of three rounds at the target will show you how far out your sights are. On most scopes one click of the adjusting dial gives either 1/4 inch or 1 cm of adjustment at 100 metres (depending on their country of manufacture), but this may vary from scope to

When zeroing, try to achieve as well supported a position as you can to enhance accuracy. A 'workmate' vice and camping stool make an excellent improvised bench rest with the addition of a sandbag or, as in this case, using a bipod.

scope. If you bought the scope new, the accompanying leaflet will tell you. If not, you may have to rely on a bit of trial and error.

Fire as many groups as necessary (taking care not to overheat the rifle barrel) until the mean point of impact (the central point of your groups of shots) is where you want it. Many stalkers like the MPI to lie about an inch above the actual point of aim to allow for fall of shot at varying ranges. Others prefer the shot to go where it was aimed, and make allowances if necessary. It is really up to you. Muntjac stalkers are very unlikely to shoot at over 100 metres, and the fall of shot is negligible at 50 metres and less than an inch at 25 metres for the common deer calibres, so there is really very little in it.

The DSC Level 1 Test - A Minimum Standard

Before you move on to a live target, the standard of shooting that you should aim to achieve is the test required for DSC Level 1. It's not too exacting, and anyone is capable of passing it with a little bit of practice. If you can't meet this standard, you really should ask yourself whether you are ready to start shooting under field conditions.

The test is in two parts. The first is on a zeroing target, and simply asks you to place three shots into a defined 4 inch circle at 100 metres. If you can't, either your rifle is not zeroed properly or you are not grouping your shots tightly enough to zero it in the first place! The shots are taken prone, and you are not permitted to use any aids to shooting that would not be available to you in the field. Sandbags are clearly out, but a bipod or a rucksack, perhaps combined with your binoculars, are perfectly acceptable.

A DSC Level 1 shooting test in progress. Note the wide variety of shooting techniques and positions.

Once you have passed the first part of the test you can move on to the second. It is shot at 100, 70 and 40 metres using a roe buck target, and again only those aids that would be available to you in the field are permitted. Two shots are fired from the prone position or a simulated high seat from 100 metres, before the firer moves to 70 metres to fire a further two shots from the sitting or kneeling position. Use of a stalking stick (or sticks) is allowed. Finally, another two rounds are fired from 40 metres from the standing position, with or without sticks as you prefer. All six shots must fall within the 'killing area' on the buck target, which is marked to be visible close up though not through your telescopic sights. It is therefore essential that you are taking the right point of aim - which is of course an important aspect of the test in the first place.

Advanced Practice
If the DSC Level 1 test is a good entry standard for the stalker, this does not mean that he should not aspire to an even higher one. Muntjac are not only our smallest species of deer, but they also tend to be the most mobile, and demand much higher standards of shooting. They do not allow you the time to test and adjust your position before taking a shot - linger too long and they will be gone!

Time spent practicing getting the rifle off your shoulder and into a shooting position is never wasted. Carrying the rifle muzzle down permits you to slip the sling off your shoulder and twist the rifle as it is brought up onto the sticks using one hand. There are other methods – do not be afraid to experiment and find the one that suits you best.

Be ready to take advantage of whatever support is available to help you shoot accurately.

Teaching yourself to shoot quickly and accurately, from whatever position is immediately available to you, is of the essence. Murphy's Law dictates that in a wood full of trees you are always several paces away from one when a deer presents itself. You have to use whatever support is available at the time, and if there is none you must create your own. Shooting without a support, particularly from standing, should be avoided wherever possible because a steady, well aimed shot is virtually impossible, hence the need to carry a good stick. It is equally important to practice getting the rifle from your shoulder and into a firing position smoothly but quickly - this can be done at home just as well as on the range. A rifle waving around in the air as the stalker contorts himself will warn the most foolish deer that something is amiss.

Try shooting from a variety of positions, as there is a world of difference between the rifle range and the woods. You will find no level, comfortable firing point when you are out stalking unless you are exceptionally lucky. As I have said elsewhere, standing will probably become your most usual shooting position, but don't neglect the possibilities offered by fallen trees, fences and the like. If you don't find shooting sitting on a flat surface comfortable enough to use in preference to kneeling when on the range, grassy banks often offer better opportunities if you are waiting in ambush. It's always worth practicing from a high seat as well. These offer very stable platforms for steady, accurate shots - but only if you are used to using them.

Use the range to become totally familiar with your rifle, and discover how it (and you) perform at varying ranges. Ballistic tables, often supplied with commercial ammunition, are a useful guide on bullet trajectories, but these will vary according to all kinds of factors in individual rifles. Furthermore, awareness of your own limitations will dictate how you shoot for real. Practice on a target will quickly show you just how difficult it is to pull off a neck shot at anything but the closest range, and hopefully convince you that the chest is a far more suitable target. Don't neglect trying a shot or two at point blank range - there may be occasions when a wounded animal may need the coup de grace, or you are called to put an animal hit by a car out of its misery. Because the scope is mounted a couple of inches higher than the rifle barrel, very close shots will hit lower than your aim. The rifle range is the place to discover exactly how far you should aim off.

Sadly, paper muntjac targets are not widely available but roe targets are. These should become your standard practice targets. Paste them onto a piece of plywood or heavy cardboard (the sort used by removal firms for their boxes are excellent), cut them out and nail a single stake to the rear end for fixing them into the ground (a stake fixed to the front will quickly become shot through). Firing at a deer target lends an element of realism to your practice, and teaches you to instinctively take the right point of aim. Keep the 'bulls eye' targets for zeroing or more deliberate practice.

Have a thought to the effects of the wind on a bullet's flight. I have heard it said that side winds have no effect on a modern, fast bullet at normal deer stalking ranges. This is patently untrue, although the effects are small to almost non-existent in light winds. Strong or gusting side winds are a different matter altogether. I have been on rifle ranges where the firers (using a wide variety of calibres) have had to aim off several inches to allow for bullet drift at 100 metres. This could mean the difference between a well-hit animal and one that is gut shot.

We all seem to go through periods when our shooting deteriorates for some reason or another. If so, a good session on the range soon puts it right. It is very easy to get complacent about stalking and neglect the range work, but it does no harm to fire a few shots at a paper target from time to time, if only to confirm zero. This not only keeps your confidence up, but reduces any margins for error when it comes to the real thing. It goes without saying that a quick session to confirm zero is always in order if you have an unexplained miss, or if the rifle or scope takes a knock.

Don't neglect the humble .22. The cost of a few shots with the deer rifle can provide for a whole afternoon with rimfire ammunition. It's excellent practice – after all, the principles are the same and all you need to do is reduce the distances you are shooting at. The only thing missing is the recoil of a centrefire rifle. If you find that you are developing a flinch or any other unhelpful habits, a session with the .22 can help you back onto the straight and narrow in no time. And it has the added attraction of being terrific fun as well!

Rifle maintenance
No section on range work would be complete without a few words on rifle maintenance. Stories abound of rifles that never get cleaned but still shoot accurately, but to be honest all of the truly excellent shots that I know have an established routine for keeping their rifles in first-class working order. True, modern ammunition and smokeless powders do not damage the barrel in the way that the old corrosive powders did, but nevertheless there will be some residue after firing. Metallic deposits from the bullet itself will also build up in time and affect accuracy if not removed. With proper care a rifle will last a lifetime and continue to shoot reliably, accurately and consistently. Occasional servicing by a qualified riflesmith will be highly beneficial if used in addition to your more regular attentions.

The occasions that might demand emergency rifle cleaning in the field are few and can be avoided with a bit of care. The simple safeguard of a piece of electrician's tape over the rifle muzzle will prevent water, dirt or debris from getting into the barrel in most instances. You will, however, find it useful to carry an emergency cleaning kit, either in your rucksack or at least available in the car. Wet or dirty barrels may result in inaccurate shooting and are a potential safety hazard. If there is any doubt about the bore of the rifle being totally clean and dry, it must be cleaned thoroughly before any shot is taken, be it at a target or a live deer.

For the sake of a small bottle of oil, screwdriver or combination tool, dry rag and sufficient flannelette or cleaning patches to completely clean, oil and dry out a barrel, you have the means to carry on stalking when otherwise you might have had to go home to do the job. A pullthrough or cleaning rod and jag completes the ensemble. Pullthroughs are convenient and take up very little space, but a rod that will break down into several sections is better as a barrel plugged with mud can be tricky to clear. A normal cleaning rod kept in the car is a helpful compromise. If you do use a pullthrough, always insert it at the breech end of the rifle and pull it through in a perfectly straight line. Pull it at an angle and you risk causing wear to the muzzle which, over time, is capable of radically affecting accuracy.

Never dump the rifle straight into its cabinet after an outing. Cleaning should always be carried out to an appropriate degree as soon as possible on your

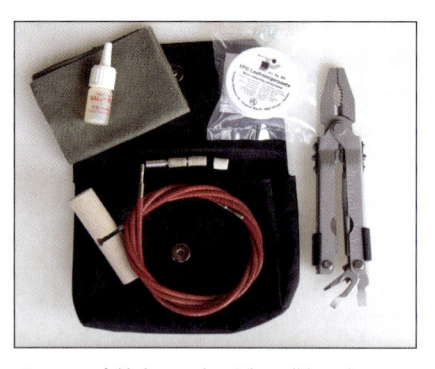

A compact field cleaning kit. The pullthrough is made of plastic coated wire, rigid enough to push obstructions such as mud or other debris out of the rifle barrel if necessary. A multi tool completes the ensemble.

Many people simply roll a piece of flannelette straight onto the jag. If you hold the flannelette against the jag as shown, then fold in first the lower corner and then the right before rolling on the rest, you will find that the two are less likely to part company halfway down the rifle barrel.

return, whether the rifle has been fired or not. At the most basic level of daily maintenance, a barrel should be cleaned out using a rod, jag and flannelette to remove any traces of damp or dust. Take care over the size of flannelette patch that you use - it is easy to jam it halfway up the barrel and nothing short of a trip to the gunsmith will get it out! Start with a small piece and work up to a size that produces a snug fit as it is pushed through.

Unless the rifle is to be left unused for some time, there is no need to oil it but it must be kept perfectly dry. The whole of the rifle should be wiped down with a lightly oiled rag, taking special care to remove any moisture or blood. Bare metal will rust in no time at all if left wet, and blood can ruin a blued finish. If the rifle has been soaked in a rain shower, make sure that it is completely dry before you put it away in the gun cabinet, and don't forget unseen areas such as the sling swivels. The sling itself can be taken off to dry, and then cleaned with saddle soap or a proprietary leather treatment. This will not only prolong its life, but prevent it from squeaking when dry (plaited slings are especially prone to this). Don't forget the scope lenses, which should be dried and polished with a proper lens cleaning cloth, taking care not to scratch the glass. Leave the lens caps off, or the flip-up caps open if you use them, while the rifle is stored.

A suitable desiccating agent, such as silica gel or one of the purpose-made dehumidifiers, inside the rifle cabinet is good insurance against the presence of moisture. Some even produce a light vapour which provides further protection.

More comprehensive cleaning needs to be carried out from time, dependent on how often the rifle is used, whether it has been fired, and how grimy it has become, but certainly not less than every few months. If any barrel fouling is difficult to remove, it can be loosened with a phosphor-bronze brush before the bore is swabbed out with a flannelette patch or wool mop soaked in a suitable solvent. There are all kinds of brands available for gun cleaning, but do take care not to get solvent anywhere on the rifle but in the bore itself. Follow the instructions on the bottle, which normally involve leaving the solvent to soak for an hour or so before it is cleaned out with successive flannelette patches until they come out clear of residue. You may be surprised at how much can be produced from a barrel that looks clean to the naked eye.

A simple home cleaning kit for maintaining your rifle. The gun stand at the back is an inexpensive plastic affair that collapses to pack flat. It is useful not just for cleaning, but also for holding the rifle securely when using a collimator or bore sighting.

A small brush can help you get at the fiddlier aspects of the rifle, such as the trigger, safety catch, chamber and action. An old toothbrush is excellent. All that the bolt usually needs is a wipe over with an oily rag, but do take care not to get any oil inside it or indeed any of the other actions as they may eventually become clogged up. Don't neglect the magazine - it's frequently overlooked - again cleaning out any dirt with a brush and paying special attention to the spring.

Always try to ensure that the stock is kept dry and clean. If it is wooden with an oiled finish, a small amount of linseed or walnut oil rubbed in well from time to time will prevent it from absorbing moisture and help to prolong its life. Varnished finishes may only need to be rubbed down with a silicone cloth, and modern plastic stocks demand even less care. Stutzen, or full stock, rifles can be particularly prone to collecting debris - run a thin sheet of paper between stock and barrel to ensure that nothing is trapped there. Anything that touches a barrel that is meant to be free-floating will affect accuracy.

It is not difficult to remove the barrel and action from the stock, allowing you to clean the areas that are not normally accessible, but I would recommend that you get someone who knows what they are doing to show you how. This need not happen often, maybe once a year or if the rifle has got particularly dirty or wet. A light smear of Vaseline or a similar grease can be used to lightly coat the underside of the barrel before it is reassembled. Great care must be taken not to get any solvent or oil onto the woodwork - not only will it ruin an oiled finish, but it will actually soften the wood if allowed to soak in. Likewise, equal care must be taken not to damage or disturb the bedding, which will have an adverse effect on accuracy.

All screws should be kept clean and tight, particularly those that secure the bedding and scope mounting. Take care not to over-tighten them, and use gunsmiths turnscrews which are less likely to damage them in the way that a normal screwdriver might. A drop of Loctite will help to keep them firmly in place.

Do take care that, every time the action is removed from the stock, or a screw is tightened, a check group should be fired as the zero of the rifle may be affected.

If a rifle is to be stored for a while, all metal surfaces should be oiled to help protect against rust. There's no need to overdo it - a very light coating is all that's needed. If I leave a rifle barrel oiled, I find it useful to plug the muzzle with the oily patch afterwards to remind me to dry it thoroughly before firing it. A dry atmosphere is essential whatever the storage facilities, and for further protection the rifle can be wrapped in specially treated paper of the sort that new rifles are supplied in. Ideally, the rifle should be stored upright in a purpose-made rest, standing on its butt, or secured horizontally in a cradle. If you need to wrap a rifle for any reason, don't use plastic bubble wrap as it may retain moisture. An old blanket is a much better alternative.

CHAPTER 6
Stalking Technique

This chapter is all about getting yourself into a position to take a shot, the shot itself, and how to follow it up. There are three basic ways of getting yourself into a position to have a chance of a shot in the first place; actively seeking out a muntjac, ambushing it as it goes about its daily life, and actually trying to bring it to you. First, though, it will pay to think about a few fundamental principles before we look at getting out onto the ground.

Camouflage & Concealment - Basic Principles
Anyone who has undergone basic military training will be familiar with the principles of camouflage and concealment - shape, shine, silhouette, shadow and the rest. With the muntjac, however, we are not trying to fool an enemy soldier. Instead we are looking to defeat the senses of an animal whose senses are finely tuned to survival, and which will be quick to spot anything unusual.

The sense of smell is very important to deer; here a buck moistens his nose to improve its scenting ability.

Human beings, with their blunted senses, cannot begin to appreciate the world of scent that most animals live in, and the importance of it to their daily lives. As it is for all deer, the sense of smell is very important to the muntjac. Just a suggestion of human scent in the woods is enough to put them on the alert, and an alert muntjac's first reaction is usually to get into cover from which it can observe without being seen.

To be successful in stalking we must take care that our scent does not reach the animal in the first place, and that means being continually aware of the wind direction.

Ideally, the wind needs to be in your face and taking the scent away behind you. A quartering wind is workable - but if the wind is coming from your back, don't expect too much luck. The truly successful stalker will not only be constantly aware of wind direction, but will come to learn those parts of the woods where the wind backs and eddies, often doing the most surprising things. Cigarette or pipe smoke is an excellent wind indicator but you should take considerable care if you must smoke when stalking, particularly in summer when the woodland floor can be a potential tinder box. A twelve inch length of white pure silk thread tied to the top end of your stalking stick will indicate the slightest breeze. Some people go to the lengths of carrying children's bubble-blowing tubs, or bags of dust, to help them assess the wind direction. Excessive? I leave it to you, but if it works I suggest that it's worth trying.

As might be expected in a creature that has evolved to exist within dense cover, hearing is also of high importance. A muntjac's ears are very mobile and swivel constantly to try and pick up any sound that is out of the ordinary. You might get away with the odd snapped twig - after all, they break for any number of reasons - but clumsy footsteps will put everything in the vicinity on the alert. Take care not to make any noises out of keeping with the woods. Metal on metal is perhaps the most obvious sign to the deer of human presence as it has no natural equivalent.

Muntjac sight does not seem to be as keen as that of, say, Scottish red deer that rely heavily on their keen eyesight to spot danger on the open hill. In fact, you can often take astonishing liberties with an animal in plain view a hundred metres or so away as long as your movements are slow and deliberate. However, that is not to say that you cannot discount the muntjac's eyes entirely. Sudden movement will attract their attention immediately, and give away your presence just as effectively as your scent or any noise that you may make.

Don't be too concerned by the colour of your clothing. Science has yet to prove that deer can see in anything but monochrome; some believe that they are actually colour-blind. It is the texture and shape of what you wear that makes you really stand out to them. A skylined human outline is obvious; with a suitable background you will blend in far more easily. The pale flesh of your

Muntjac – Managing an Alien Species

Moving quietly and slowly through the woods, taking care to keep the wind in your face and stopping frequently to scan around you with the binoculars, will greatly increase your chances of detecting a deer before it sees you

A suitable mask and gloves are essential to conceal your face and hands, and especially the movement involved in the constant use of binoculars

face and hands needs to be covered, especially the latter which are mobile as you use your binoculars, move hanging branches out of your path, or whatever. Taking these facts into consideration, and moving slowly with a mind to your outline, will allow you to get very close to your quarry if you do so with immense care.

Never forget that the muntjac is a small animal that is used to living in thick cover. It habitually carries its head low for a reason - to help it see through it. You are used to a line of vision placed several feet higher up, and it is easy to forget that your bottom half might be visible for a long way while the top half is concealed by branches. It pays to get down and look at the muntjac perspective from time to time, even if it can be sore work for your back!

Muntjac are small deer that habitually hold their heads low – as a result they are seeing under cover that you cannot see through, or over

A Seasonal Approach
The other five species of deer found in Britain have very specific behaviour defined by the turning of the seasons, and will give birth, rut and form herds at the same times year on year. This is largely governed by increasing and decreasing daylight hours. So how, then, can we adopt a seasonal approach to stalking the very aseasonal muntjac when the only aspects of its life that occur at specific times of the year are antler growth and coat change? The truth is that other factors will affect how it behaves, in particular the climate and the growth cycles of the cover and food sources that it depends upon. Of these, it's mainly the food sources that you need to give special attention.

Spring is the time of new growth, which will be eagerly sought out after the lean months of winter. As a concentrate selector, the muntjac will be more inclined to travel in search of buds and shoots which are rich sources of quality forage. Where agricultural and game crops exist in close proximity to cover, significant damage may occur along the edges of it - though never to far out where instant refuge is not easily available. The muntjac does not like to spend too much time in the open, especially during daylight. As this is a season of wet weather, damp ground will more readily show the dainty slots of muntjac and show you where they, and not rabbits and hares, are responsible. Now is the time to position a portable high seat to overlook the main areas.

This is also the time of year when quietly moving about the woods on foot can pay dividends. By June the woodland floor will have grown up to the point where observation is all but impossible, so take advantage of being able to see a respectable distance around you. The muntjac will move at any time of day in places which are undisturbed by human activity, but you can often catch him on his way back into denser cover after feeding on the field edges during the hours of darkness.

Things get more difficult during the summer months. The woods can seem like primary jungle at this time, and you have very few chances of seeing more than a few feet in places. It's not impossible, though. High seats or other vantage points that cover track junctions provide you with chances to intercept patrolling animals, although a bit of judicious work with the pruning saw may be necessary if you are to have workable fields of fire.

Whilst some muntjac will decamp to live in standing crops once they are high enough to provide a feeling of security, they will not stay there permanently and will emerge to seek other feeding areas. If the farmer has left a strip of bare land between crop and wood edge, the deer will find this a reasonably secure place to be and move along it freely.

Autumn is a time of plenty. Nuts, berries, windfall fruit and fungi are plentiful and any spot which offers these will be visited by the foraging muntjac. Like most animals, they will be seeking to put on condition for the leaner months ahead, and will be feeding heavily and selectively from the abundance. It's worth taking note of such places and giving them special attention. The deer will be travelling extensively within their home ranges as they seek out the highest quality food and, with woodland growth receding, you will be in a better position to spot them.

You'd think that winter is the best time of year to spot muntjac, as the cover dies back and the woodland floor is left largely bare. This is not necessarily so. Many of the food sources have now disappeared, and the deer will be wherever the remaining ones are. This will very likely be the bramble patches which provide food and cover the year round. Once again, the portable high seat is very useful to cover any hot spots. Ivy becomes an important foodstuff at this time of year, and any trees or branches brought down by winter gales, making previously unreachable leaves available, are worth watching.

Strips of land between standing crops and the woodland edge are frequently used by deer; high seats or impromptu ambushes can both be productive.

Brambles provide an important source of food and cover throughout the year

Pheasant feeders, with a ready supply of spilt grain, can be very attractive to deer

Not all wild muntjac take readily to salt licks, although captive animals like this one will use them regularly

Any other sources will not be missed; pheasant feeders in places where there are organised shoots can be magnets for the muntjac, and a good look at any muddy patches around them will show tracks where the deer are using them. I know of one stalker who enjoys great success by rattling the lids of the metal bins used as pheasant feeding stations, then standing quietly a short way off to await the deer that come soon afterwards to look for spilt grain.

Whilst Continental-style feeding stations, maintained to encourage deer numbers at higher levels than the environment could naturally support, have no place under British conditions, you can consider establishing feeding points to encourage muntjac to come out of cover and within range. Accordingly to seasonal availability many foodstuffs are attractive to muntjac. Windfall apples, collected earlier in the year and stored for the purpose, are popular but do not seem to be eaten until they are starting to rot. Presumably this makes them easier for the muntjac to break up and digest. Root crops do not seem to be quite as effective in general, although carrots can be popular. If you can beg strawberry plants - leaves, berries and all - from a commercial farmer at the end of the growing season, this can be a very effective attractant. Salt licks are occasionally used by muntjac, but some individual animals appear to take to them more readily than others and the attraction does not seem to be universal.

Do not be afraid to experiment with whatever is available. It is the work of a few minutes to put something out; the trick is to keep it replenished and get the deer used to visiting it. Feeding is not the ultimate solution to reducing muntjac numbers, but it can be a very useful addition to your methods.

Locating & Spotting

There are two old adages that hold very true when you are trying to find your quarry. The first is that you can't shoot what you can't see. The second is that you are just as likely to see a deer where you are as where you are going.

Is there a best time of day for finding muntjac out of cover? There is no hard and fast answer. In areas where they are undisturbed, muntjac will move and feed freely at any time. I have seen them feeding on the banks of the M4 motorway on the edge of Reading as I have driven past at midday. In areas where they are more harried, however, muntjac are likely to become more nocturnal in their habits and a dawn and dusk approach is more likely to be successful. My personal preference is early morning stalking, but there are many who find that they are just as successful during the last hour or so of daylight. Take your pick and find what works best for you – quite often work and family considerations will play a large part in your decision!

A friend of mine has stalked the same area, which holds muntjac and roe, for almost three years now. He is an experienced stalker, and makes a solid contribution towards the annual roe cull. Yet for a long while he refused to believe that the area holds muntjac. The other members of his deer group put him in the best high seats, set him to stalk the most productive areas, even moved the woods for him. All to no avail. Everyone else was bringing muntjac carcases in, but not him. One day he went out for an afternoon, walked around a corner, saw two muntjac bucks in plain view and shot them both. That was nine or ten months ago – he hasn't seen a muntjac since. He is still stalking with a picture of roe in his mind, and seems incapable of adjusting that mental picture to include muntjac. He freely admits that the two he shot were down to luck, pure and simple.

Muntjac are constantly on the move when not ruminating, and you have a fair chance of seeing them at any time of the day in areas where they are not too disturbed.

Learn to look for shapes and colours, rather than the whole deer

The fact is that if you are used to stalking a larger species of deer your eyes are 'set' at the wrong height and you automatically look in the wrong places. The muntjac is much lower at the shoulder than a roe, and shorter-legged in comparison. To add to the difference he tends to hold his head low rather than erect. Very well, my friend was particularly unlucky as we often see muntjac flitting across the path in front of us when stalking even if we do not get a chance of a shot, but by looking for something else he simply wasn't giving himself a chance in the first place.

Don't look for a whole deer – they are not usually obliging enough to offer the stalker a picture postcard view of their whole selves. What we must have in out minds are colours and shapes. The muntjac's presence is often only given away by the 'V' formed by the ears, the horizontal line of a back, or even just the glint of an eye. A patch of white may be the rear of an animal feeding away from you, or a small movement caught out of the corner of your eye may be the flick of an ear. You have to check everything unusual through the binoculars. Nine times out of ten it may be nothing – but suddenly the investigation of an odd shape, colour or line that doesn't seem right brings the entire animal into sharp focus.

Get used to carrying a mental picture of your quarry in your head. Be aware of size, shape and colour, and the fact that the latter is different when the animal is in winter and summer coats. Look especially hard for fragments of the whole picture. Check out everything unusual, or which strikes you as slightly out of place as you pass through the woods. And remember that movement can be your greatest ally – as long as it is the animal that is moving, and you spot

These targets, the left hand one cut down to represent a couched deer, show how easy it is for a muntjac to hide behind sparse cover

it first. And finally, don't forget to use your ears. A barking muntjac can go on for a long time, and may guide you in to where it is.

Stalking
Strictly speaking, I suppose that the term 'stalking' describes the active and stealthy pursuit of deer, but we tend to apply it to all aspects of hunting deer with a rifle in this country. The American expression 'still hunting' may be misleading at first sight, but is actually a first class description of what we are trying to achieve as we move about the woods.

Movement is the biggest giveaway, both of the presence of you and of your quarry. You are bigger and clumsier than the deer, and on its home ground. You have poorer hearing, weaker eyesight and virtually no sense of smell. It follows that you must use what few advantages you have to gain the upper hand. You do not have to move about the woods as part of your daily life, but the deer must. Patience and observation are therefore the keys to success.

All movement needs to be painstaking. Your eyes must be everywhere – and not just where you are going. Don't expect your quarry to run off the moment it sees you coming. Jim Corbett, the celebrated hunter of tigers in India during the early decades of the 20th century and an acute observer of jungle life, himself commented that muntjac tend to stand stock still if they believe that you have not seen them. A deer in low cover may well let you go past if it is convinced that it has not been seen, then stand up to reassure itself that you are leaving, so look behind you frequently. If you are stalking well, you may find that a patrolling deer will cross behind or to the side of you in any case.

Muntjac will frequently freeze in cover and let you walk past if they believe that they have not been spotted

You must be constantly aware of where you are putting your feet. In the quiet of the woods, a breaking twig can sound like a rifle shot and put everything in the vicinity on the alert. Hopefully you are wearing footwear that lets you feel the shape of the ground beneath you. I suppose that bare feet are ideal, but I've never been drawn to such an extreme! Gravelled tracks or carpets of dried leaves are a stalker's nightmare. Mossy patches and the like can be very useful, allowing silent passage though otherwise noisy areas. But remember, the faster you travel, the more noise you are likely to make.

If your surroundings allow it, get off the beaten tracks and paths and into the woods themselves. Try to avoid crossing large open spaces like the plague; all they do is make you more obvious to anything observing from within cover. Try instead to move short distances between anything that will break your outline up – trees, bushes or whatever. And always move slowly, a few paces at a time.

I can't labour the point enough - take your time. However slowly you think you are moving, chances are that you are going too fast. Force yourself to slow down, and stop frequently. Lean against a tree or sit on a stump and simply observe. You have a better chance of seeing something by sitting still than by rushing from place to place. Do everything – turning your head, raising and lowering binoculars – slowly. Movement attracts attention, so make it your ally, not the deer's. If you have taken my advice and invested in a high quality pair of binoculars, don't waste them - use them often. They are your greatest advantage. You'd be amazed at what the naked eye misses and find that, more often than not, the deer are coming to you, not vice versa.

Although muntjac tend to feed 'on the hoof', snipping a mouthful here and there as they patrol, occasionally you'll get the opportunity for a more classic stalk – perhaps of an animal feeding on a particularly tempting patch of new growth or fallen fruit. Again, take your time and don't go blundering in. Be prepared to get down on your hands and knees, or crawl on your belly if

Use your binoculars frequently to sweep even the most insignificant cover

Muntjac blend in remarkably well with their surroundings, and very frequently it is only movement that gives their presence away.

necessary. Although you can't hang around - your quarry may not be there for long before it moves on - rest assured that if it sees, hears or smells you it will be away in a flash anyway.

Plan your approach, keeping the wind in your face as much as possible, and always be on the alert for other deer and animals that might give the game away. The clattering flight of pigeons disturbed from their perches can be a particular curse in woodland, and the quacking of duck flushing from a stream or small pond can seem enough to wake the dead. And if you are aware of the chattering alarm call of a blackbird, you can be sure that the deer are too.

Actively stalking deer, if you are doing it well, is mentally exhausting. Even if you only cover a few hundred metres in the course of an outing lasting a couple of hours, you need to remain completely alert throughout. Chances can come at any moment – especially with a quarry as active and constantly mobile as the muntjac. Switch off for a moment, and an opportunity may be lost. If only I had a pound for every animal shot at a point when I had all but given up hope of seeing one – and then again, a pound for every one that I disturbed as I returned to the car, off-guard and convinced that I was about to go home empty-handed!

Don't be tempted to shoot from a vehicle, however tempting the target may be. Not only is this lazy and bad practice, it is also potentially dangerous and largely illegal. All species of deer will normally stand and let a vehicle go by in areas where they are used to seeing them on a regular basis. Even should the vehicle stop, they will often remain there as long as they do not feel that they are under any immediate threat. When a deer bolts at the first sign of a motor vehicle, it is a clear sign that it has learnt to associate it with danger – and a good indication to you that something dodgy is going on out there.

High Seats

High seats are a very useful - if not invaluable - tool in the muntjac manager's armoury. In the stalking of a deer which is constantly on the move when feeding, they permit you to let it come to you rather than have to seek it out. Looking down into and over vegetation, your vision is enhanced, you have a stable shooting platform to take a shot from, and (very importantly) shooting downwards increases the chances of a safe backstop for the bullet.

As deer rarely look up, by being several feet above ground level the stalker has a better chance of staying unseen. He also has a reduced chance of being winded by the deer as his scent originates higher. Most importantly of all, he is static and is less likely to give himself away by movement. A high seat is an excellent means of ensuring that a visiting stalker stays put where you left him, only shoots within restricted arcs and does not blunder around the woods out of your sight!

Inevitably, there are a few disadvantages associated with high seats. A high seat can quickly become redundant in a quickly growing new plantation. It will need to be maintained regularly, not least with Health & Safety regulations in mind, as wood will rot and metal will rust. Do not forget that the presence of high seats advertises not only the presence of stalkers in an age of delicate sensitivities towards deer management, but also the presence of deer themselves to poachers. Vandalism is also a major problem in some areas.

Give careful thought to the future before committing time and resources to building a permanent seat. A fast-growing conifer plantation quickly reduced the effectiveness of this one.

Both the estate and the stalker may well have a legal liability if there is an accident. If a member of the public - or a poacher - climbs up and subsequently injures themselves, irrespective as to whether they have the right to be there or not, the owner of the seat is likely to be held liable . It is possible to limit public access by building a removable ladder that can be taken away when the seat is not in use. All seats left unattended should be marked with suitable warning signs and their construction and use must comply with Industrial and Health & Safety laws at all times. It is strongly recommended that you keep a register of your seat locations, individual identifications, maintenance & repairs. Serviceability inspections ought to be carried out at least twice a year, and any seats deemed unsafe must be removed.

A portable high seat is an excellent short-term option, especially if you are new to a piece of ground and have yet to learn the 'hot spots'. They are usually of the 'lean-to' variety and can be switched easily from place to place, especially when attention needs to be paid to problem areas or when undergrowth renders their use impossible. They can also be used to 'prove' a location before you go to the time and trouble of erecting a permanent seat.

A commercially made portable high seat in use.

The same seat folded down for transporting.

Do take care with portable seats though. They tend to be expensive and, being portable, are easily stolen, so insurance and a stout chain and padlock securing them to a tree are essential. Their lightness also means that you need to take special care in siting them to be as stable as possible, both for accurate shooting and for the safety of the user.

Permanent seats can be costly to build and maintain, but are a great asset if correctly sited in areas where they will be useful for the years to come. They should only be considered once you know the ground well and are able to site them where they will be of true value – they should never be considered as the 'magic ingredient' that is guaranteed to improve stalking success.

There is any number of designs for seats, and if you are building your own the only limit is your own ingenuity. Alternatively, a number of designs are commercially available. A 12' aluminium ladder can be converted into a lean-to portable seat with the careful addition of a bucket seat, shooting rail and rope or chain for securing it to the tree to prevent it falling over. At the other end of the spectrum are German-style shooting boxes, ultra-comfortable with sleeping areas.

An enclosed box high seat. Although time-consuming to erect, such a seat is warm and dry and conceals the movements of a fidgeting stalker. Note the warning sign attached to the right hand side of the ladder

Don't discount low seats – simple boxes that can be constructed at ground level wherever a suitable vantage point is offered by the lie of the land.. They can range from quite sophisticated shed-like arrangements with slits through which the stalker can observe and shoot, to a simple 'v' formed from two pallets set on their sides. Even a military surplus camouflage net strung between two poles can serves as a very useful temporary hide, easily carried and erected in a likely spot. They are often a very practical alternative where there is no suitable tree to lean a conventional high seat against. You need to be particularly careful about siting with a suitable backstop for the bullet – a low seat which from which you cannot shoot safely is a waste of time.

Whatever you opt for, remember that you will want to be able to sit still in it for up to two or three hours at a time without fidgeting, and shoot accurately and safely when the time comes. Stability and sound construction should be your watchwords - I have sat in high seats ranging from the mildly alarming to the utterly terrifying, and some which swayed so much in the wind that I would never have attempted a shot given the chance.

If you are building a seat from wood, never use raw 'green' timber cut on site, as it will quickly rot and become dangerous. Creosoted or pressure-treated timber is better, but will still need regular inspection (any supports dug into the ground on a permanent seat will need special checking for deterioration). Larch and other conifers are particularly useful but birch is especially prone to rotting and may break without warning. Peeled wood helps to prevent rapid deterioration. All wood should be drilled for nails to prevent splitting, and rungs set into uprights and wired against breakage. Chicken mesh should be stapled to all surfaces that are stood on to help prevent accidental slipping. Metals are useful, particularly aluminium, but can be noisy if not cladded.

Many high seats are valueless as scant attention has been paid to their siting. Once a permanent seat is built, it may be virtually impossible to move to another site. By giving a bit of thought to location, the usefulness of the seat can be greatly enhanced.

Thinks about local factors, such as the prevailing wind in your area. Will it carry your scent into the ground that you are overlooking? Also consider the direction of the rising and setting sun which might blind you at key times for deer activity. You will need to get into the seat easily and quietly, so access (preferably out of sight of the killing area) is important. Ideally, the approach route should be downwind of the seat. Once in the seat, you should ensure that there is a suitable background to prevent you from being easily spotted by the deer in silhouette.

Next, consider the area that you intend to be shooting into. Tree branches, bare in winter, will sprout leaves in spring and may obscure your view. It is also surprising how a bare woodland floor can produce vegetation that would conceal a bull elephant in summer! Young plantations offering easy visibility can quickly become impenetrable and, in these cases, a less permanent seat construction would be wise. You might also want to consider cutting fire lanes and trimming branches to ensure good visibility - don't forget to get permission from the landowner or forester first. While you are at it, find out future plans for the woodland in question - there is nothing more annoying than, having gone to the trouble of erecting a state-of-the-art permanent seat, to find that the entire area is felled six months later!

Don't forget the deer themselves. Is the area actually attractive to them, and if so is it on a permanent or seasonal basis? Ideally you will want to overlook regularly used movement lines or browsing areas - track junctions or clearings are often excellent places offering good visibility. Try to find places where the deer feel secure and are less likely to flit from cover to cover.

And once you are in the seat and waiting for a deer to show itself, do sit still and keep your movements to the absolute minimum. Some people, having heard that deer rarely look up, seem to think that they are invisible. This is patently not so. Muntjac, especially, come from a part of the world where danger can frequently come from above and it would be foolish to believe that this has disappeared entirely from their inbred consciousness after a mere hundred years or so in this country. And although your scent is several feet off the ground, remember that if you leave any kit (such as your sticks or rucksack) at the base of the seat your scent will still be on them – take them off the ground with you.

A free-standing high seat allows for siting even where there are no suitable trees for support. This double seater is ideal for guests or stalkers under training. It would benefit from a coat of drab-coloured paint, and a suitable background to stop anyone in it from being silhouetted against the sky

A wooden seat thoughtfully sited at the junction of three tracks. As summer vegetation dies back, visibility will improve even further.

View from a woodland seat in early spring. Although the stalker has good visibility, there is sufficient cover for the deer to feel secure as they move about the woods.

Anything which makes you comfortable is a bonus – high seats can be utterly miserable in cold or wet weather, so dress appropriately. A small square of foam sheet can turn a hard, wet seat from an instrument of torture into something much easier to tolerate during your vigil. If you find that you are easily bored, a miniature radio with ear phones helps – but leave one ear clear so that you can pick up the sounds of the woods around you. I have even seen a pair of car wing mirrors fixed so as to give the sitter all round views – not as silly an idea as it might seem, as it saves you from constantly having to turn to look around. A very innovative way, in fact, of reducing unnecessary movement.

And finally, give a thought to the public. Try to site your seat well away from public footpaths, and certainly out of sight of curious eyes. Make sure that you are aware of any rights of way in the area - not only to ensure safe shooting, but also to minimise the chance of coming into contact with the public. People are very bad at sticking to defined tracks, may often choose to investigate odd sights and sounds, and often turn up in the strangest places doing the oddest things! Never forget that an unattended high seat is an open invitation to any passing thief, vandal, poacher or courting couple - and you are likely to be held liable when any of them fall out of it.

Calling

The technique of calling roe bucks during the rut, largely developed on the Continent, is now widely practised in this country. It is based on attracting bucks, or the does that they are attending, by a series of calls which tend to imitate receptive does looking for a mate, a doe hard pressed by an over-amorous buck, or a kid calling for its mother. Calling for roe is accordingly only really effective during the relatively short period of the roe rut in late July and early to mid August.

As we have already seen, there is no set period for the muntjac rut so why, then, is calling for them not more widely practised throughout the year? The fact is that there is no widely developed technique as yet available to the stalker even though there is no doubt that muntjac do respond to calls. The key to calling muntjac is to remember that they are largely responding out of curiosity rather than being driven by sexual urges, and to direct your approach accordingly.

Many a roe stalker has had muntjac respond to calls intended to tempt in a roe buck during the rut, and a number are now using them quite deliberately for muntjac. The most effective of the commercially-produced calls is probably the 'Buttolo', a rubber bulb that is squeezed in the hand to produce a variety of squeaks. In fact, any roe call that produces the 'fiep' of a receptive doe is liable to tempt a muntjac - of either sex. Interestingly, heavily pregnant does are just as likely to respond as those showing no signs of pregnancy, bucks or immature animals. All are liable to bark at the caller as they come to investigate.

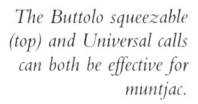

The Buttolo squeezable (top) and Universal calls can both be effective for muntjac.

If you opt to try for muntjac using a roe call, there is one thing that you ought to think about first. Calling outside the rut also serves to educate the roe on your ground to the fact that humans make these noises as well as their own kind, and you may well find that the technique quickly becomes less effective as the years progress. In areas that do not hold roe, or where calling is not important as a method of managing the latter, this consideration is not so important but should be borne in mind. A 'halfway house' might be to restrict calling outside the roe rut to a few denser corners of your stalking area which are particularly favoured by the local muntjac population. Whatever your approach, don't overdo it.

Barking apart, there is no real evidence to suggest that a muntjac doe in oestrus will attempt - vocally - to persuade a buck to join her so it is more likely that any response to artificial calling is more out of curiosity. This curiosity can be exploited. Vermin controllers often report a response to squeaking intended to summon a fox. Remember, though, if you do squeak in a muntjac when shooting foxes, that many of the calibres of rifle popular for fox control are not legal for shooting deer.

There is plenty of room for experimentation with other techniques. F Spencer Chapman was a soldier and keen naturalist who spent the Second World War in Malaysia behind Japanese lines. He often hunted muntjac with the local guerrillas. In the book of his experiences, 'The Jungle is Neutral', he notes that they could be lured in to within gunshot by splitting a small piece of bamboo and using it to create a piercing scream. The *kijang* (the local name for muntjac) would reply with a bark and come to the call. Although the *kijang* is a subspecies of Indian muntjac, as opposed to the Chinese variety that we have in Britain, this demands further investigation. Any method that tips the balance into our favour is definitely worth a try.

It is no accident that the muntjac also known as the barking deer. The bark of a muntjac can be described as terrier-like and can be imitated with practice. Barking is an important form of communication between muntjac for a variety of reasons other than alarm - the stalker who can imitate the bark can often persuade an animal to come and see off an interloper, investigate the cause of disturbance, or at least give its position away by responding. As calls can be repeated for up to an hour, this can offer the chance of a real test of stalking skills as the stalker moves carefully to locate the animal itself. It is believed that does in oestrus are especially vocal, and as this may be the muntjac equivalent of the roe doe *fieping*, there is always the chance of calling in an interested buck.

Sound recordings can be easily accessed on the Internet, and nothing beats hearing the real thing. On any ground with a healthy muntjac population there will be no shortage of animals ready to demonstrate to you.

Don't be afraid to experiment. If the deer can be persuaded to investigate a noise that is not human to their ears, any number of sounds are capable of being effective and the shooting market offers all kinds of calls designed to attract other species. There is a small fortune waiting for the first person to produce a specific and effective muntjac call commercially.

Whatever method you choose, be ready for close and quick encounters. It is highly unlikely that you will be able to tempt a muntjac fully into the open, so choose your ground carefully - a small glade or clearing with at least 30m view into cover is a start. Beyond this the cover needs to be quite thick, otherwise the animal may not feel secure enough to be tempted to investigate, but you must not be placed where the animal can see you easily and does not have to leave shelter to find out what is making the noise. Indeed, sometimes you can get a positive approach over quite a distance of open area. Make sure that you break up your outline by standing or sitting with your back to a tree or dense bush, have a mind to the wind direction as a deer that can smell you will not respond, and be sure of the backstop for a bullet in advance. Chances are that you will not have the luxury of time for careful consideration when the moment comes. Likewise it is prudent to have your rifle at the ready, on your stalking sticks or similar support, so that movement in bringing it to bear is minimal. A face veil and gloves, coupled with suitable camouflage clothing, are essential. If you use a variable-power telescopic sight, it is often wise to take it down to minimum magnification.

Choose your ground carefully when calling, allowing sufficient cover for the deer to feel secure while offering you the chance of a safe shot.

Be prepared for quick encounters when calling; your quarry is unlikely to stay in the open for long

Technique varies, but the key seems to be not to overdo it initially. Using your chosen call (general consensus is that the Buttolo squeezable model works best), make half a dozen or so squeaks and then keep still and quiet. The squeaks can be quite loud, but avoid using the double tone that you get if you squeeze the Buttolo call too hard. The plaintive call of a fawn in distress can also be effective, and seems to attract muntjac of both sexes and all age groups, not just nursing does.

Don't give up if there is no immediate reaction. Something may have come to investigate the noise but is not curious enough to leave cover yet. After a few more minutes, try a few more squeaks. This is often enough to tempt an animal into stepping out of cover temporarily. This may be your only chance before it decides to leave, hence the need to set yourself up for a quick, safe shot. Sometimes you will find yourself barked at; reply with the call, and hopefully the animal will be lured in closer to investigate. Once you have a response, you can use the call quite frequently and aggressively, and watch the reaction to it.

Do not be shy of calling from a high seat. Although deer can pinpoint the location of sounds with remarkable accuracy, the fact that you are several feet off the ground does not seem to make a noticeable difference. The height will be especially useful in helping you to spot an approaching animal, as well as keeping your scent off the ground and allowing you to bring your rifle to bear with less chance of being spotted.

A doe, clearly suspicious, barks at the caller

Finally, be patient. Although some animals may charge in like express trains, others are just as likely to come quietly and cautiously to satisfy their curiosity. A doe that has left its fawn hidden in cover nearby may be especially quick to respond, and of course here it is important to identify the fact. Choose your location, try your call and then stay still and silent for a good fifteen minutes or so before moving on. If something does turn up, you must always be ready to make a rapid decision over whether or not to shoot, then to be quick and accurate.

Calling does not always work, but it is intensely exciting when it does. Practice and confidence seem to be the key ingredients for success. But I must warn you – the strongest reaction to calling is often from a doe who has a fawn hidden nearby, so be careful to identify your target carefully before you shoot.

Moving
Muntjac can be moved to the rifle, but I'll say at the start that it is not easy to persuade them to leave their preferred strongholds. Note also that I am using the word 'moved' rather than 'driven' – forget all ideas of a formal line of beaters driving the woods as if for pheasant as it simply won't work. As I have said before, muntjac are just as likely to sit tight as move if they think that they have not been spotted or if they can get away with it. They are more likely to slip away quietly if they are not being driven hard, and therefore the better approach is to move the woods gently rather than attempt to force animals to

flee ahead of a beating line. Nor are they inclined to go far in any case; any observer at a pheasant shoot in muntjac country will testify to their preference to break back through the line rather than go forward obligingly.

The most productive way of moving muntjac is placing a few rifles strategically in high seats or at vantage points, and for a small number of individuals to 'stir up' the woods around them. Safety is always paramount, and for that reason everyone involved must be totally familiar with the lie of the land and the positioning of those doing the shooting. Thought needs to be given to such diverse matters as action to be taken if a deer goes off wounded, what the signal is to stop and return to a rendezvous, or any kind of emergency. Walkie-talkie radios or mobile telephones can help to keep everyone in touch.

The aim of moving muntjac is to persuade the animals to travel quietly about the woods, hopefully offering the stalker a chance of a shot. Excessive noise or haste will be counter-productive.

High visibility jackets allow walkers to be easily seen

I strongly recommend that the walkers do not carry rifles, no matter what the temptation 'just in case I get a chance of a shot' - this takes one very large potential for accidents out of the equation. Instead, the walkers should approach the area to be moved from upwind so that their scent gets into it well in advance of them. This will give the deer added incentive to slip away, hopefully within shot of the static rifles. Dogs are useful, but need to be under close control. The walkers are not trying to move stealthily, not are they keeping a straight beating line and trying to drive all before them. The rifles need to be aware of their locations at all times, and here high-visibility jackets (of the kind worn by road or building site workers) are very useful.

The rifles, in their turn, must be totally aware of the arcs in which they may shoot and where everyone else is. Once they are in place, it is sensible to leave a period of time for the woods to settle down before the walkers move in.

Quite often there will be an opportunity for a shot before that point, and this will itself create a degree of disturbance that will assist in the aim. Once proceedings have started, a patch of woodland can be disturbed from several directions in a morning or afternoon before calling things to a close.

Moving a wood can be productive, but by the same token it can be very disappointing. It is certainly no replacement for conventional stalking and high seat use in keeping numbers down. Don't do it too often, or the deer will get used to it and eventually retreat into the thickest areas of cover and refuse to come out at the first sign of disturbance. And I cannot stress enough – always have a mind to safety. Stalking is at its safest when the stalker is solitary. If there are to be several stalkers in one wood, it makes sense that they are kept static in high seats or other fixed positions –and that they know precisely where each other is.

The Shot
At last the moment has finally arrived and there's a muntjac in front of you. This will probably come as a bit of surprise, as the opportunities to locate and stalk muntjac in the classic manner are very few and far between. If you're lucky, you'll be sitting in a high seat with your rifle ready to hand, or you might have stalked in to get a clear shot with the rifle already off your shoulder. Chances are, though, the animal will have suddenly appeared as you move quietly through the woods. It may even be staring at you, wondering what you are and if you pose a threat. Now is not the time for sudden movements. From this point on, and whatever position you find yourself in, everything that you do must be slow and deliberate, preferably with the animal looking in any direction but yours, as you get your rifle into the aim. You can get way with a great deal even if the animal is looking directly at you, but move quickly and it will be gone.

Don't try to get into a fancy, more comfortable position unless you have found an animal that is feeding static. More likely it will be on the move, and you will lose the opportunity if you waste time. It is not an accident that muntjac stalkers need to practice shooting from standing! Use whatever support is to hand. It seems that the nearest tree will always be a few paces away, and you will be very grateful of the stick that you have taken to carrying whenever you are stalking.

As you are getting into a shooting position, a number of questions need to be going through your head. First and foremost, is the shot safe? Without a backstop to receive the bullet when it exits the animal (or, heaven forbid, misses it) it can go on for a couple more miles with fatal consequences. You can't rely on trees or other cover to stop or break up the bullet. Take care of ricochet hazards for the same reason. Rocks or metalled roads will deflect a bullet

Never consider a shot without a good backstop to receive the bullet

A much safer alternative

easily. Have you got a clear shot at the target, or are there twigs or plants in the way which might cause deflection and spoil your aim? Even grass stems are capable of causing deflection. And, of course, is the animal shootable in the first place? Be especially wary of large, slim does, where there is a strong chance that you will end up orphaning a dependant fawn.

At this point you may experience what is known as 'buck fever'. Even experienced stalkers are not totally immune to it. The excitement of the moment (not really surprising, given all the concentration and effort that has gone in to creating it) causes increased heart rate and shaking hands, making a properly aimed shot impossible. In these circumstances you simply cannot shoot and risk wounding the animal. You have no option but to hold your fire and wait for the shaking to subside. When you are ready, ease the safety catch off and do exactly what you have been doing in practice on the rifle range. If you lose the chance of a shot - never mind, the animal will be there another day and you will not suffer the anguish of a lost beast.

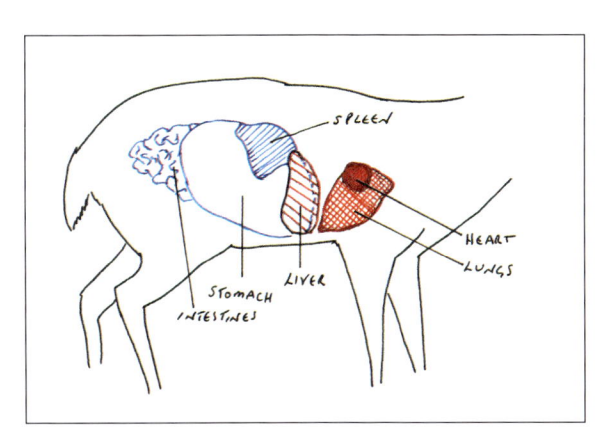

Positions of the major organs. A hit in the heart or lungs, or the major blood vessels that surround them, is quickly fatal. A liver wound is equally so, but there is a high possibility that the stomach may be ruptured and the carcase contaminated by its contents.

You will normally be aiming for a shot into the 'boiler room', namely the heart and lungs. This gives you the biggest area on the target where a hit will be immediately fatal, and allows you some small margin for error. If the animal is not standing broadside to you, wait for it to turn. A shot into the chest of one directly facing you will pass straight through the body, rupturing the stomach and tainting the carcase. Although the neck shot is an alternative if the body is obscured by cover, you need to be close enough for complete accuracy and fully confident in your shooting ability. The neck of a small animal like the muntjac is a very narrow target, and you must hit the vertebrae. A misplaced neck shot has the potential to go through the animal's windpipe without bringing it down, so this is a shot best avoided by all but the most competent marksmen.

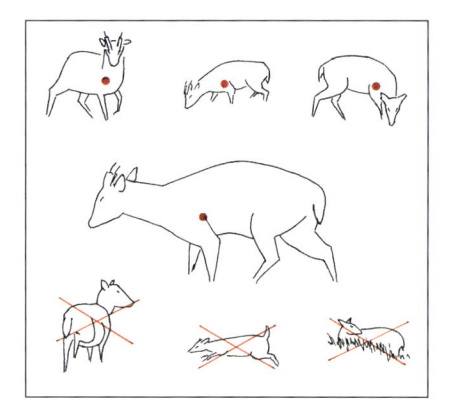

Points of aim. Look for a broadside or quartering target. You should not shoot at an animal going away from you or one that is moving. Attempts to guess at the point of aim on an animal obscured by vegetation are likely to result in a deflected or misplaced shot.

The heart and lungs are the most suitable target area. The neck is not only a smaller target, but is also more likely to move at the wrong moment.

Don't shoot at a moving animal – wait for it to stop. Once you are ready to fire, a sharp whistle may cause it to halt and look in your direction (although I frequently find that muntjac will ignore a whistle completely). A squeak from a call if you are carrying one will be more effective – sometimes it will even bring an animal that has walked into cover back into view. Saying 'stop' or 'oi' loudly enough to the animal to hear you (but not shouting) will almost invariably stop it in its tracks, but having heard a human voice it will be poised for flight and unlikely to stay around for long. You must be prepared for a quick, well-aimed shot.

Never, never attempt a head shot. The head of a deer is very mobile and the proportion of it that results in a fatal hit is relatively small. It only takes the shot to be slightly out for the animal to go off with a smashed jaw and linger on in

Ideally, the perfect target is a broadside and static animal

Never attempt a head shot. Wait for a clear shot at the heart and lung area.

extreme pain for a long time. You will not get the chance for a second shot. Fancy trick shooting has no place in practical stalking and should never be attempted against a living target. It is more likely to result in a wounded animal escaping. Save it for the rifle range.

All that is left now is to get a good, steady sight picture on your selected point of aim and squeeze the trigger. It should almost be a surprise when the rifle goes off. Many stalkers confess to never being truly aware of firing the shot until it's all over.

Immediately after firing you should reload, preferably quickly enough that the working of the rifle bolt merges with the sound of the shot. The animal may need a second shot, and you never know what else might be disturbed and appear in front of you. Resist the temptation to rush in as you are better placed where you are if a second shot is needed.

Reaction to Shot

A heart- or lung-shot muntjac will usually fall where it is hit, but occasionally one will run on you. Although a muntjac is a relatively small deer, it is dangerous to assume that they fall readily to a bullet. I have seen a mortally-wounded muntjac run almost 100 metres when hit in the lungs, and as far as 50 metres when heart-shot (in one case with a heavy 150 grain round from a .308). The flight reflex is strong and can take over even when an animal is technically dead on its feet, especially when small, fast bullets are involved or if the deer is on the alert at the time. As a muntjac is seldom far from cover, it pays to understand the reactions to a hit on different parts of the body so that the animal can be followed up and the carcase recovered.

Hopefully your target will drop as if poleaxed when hit in a vital area. Beware, though, for a shot that creases the spine will cause temporary paralysis and also have this effect. If a deer seems to be dead but then starts to struggle to its feet, you will need to be prepared to shoot again quickly. If not, it may be up and away in no time.

If a shot deer rears up, jumps slightly or lashes out with its rear legs before rushing off, often with the head held low, you can be fairly certain of a good hit in the heart and lungs and can reasonably expect to find it lying dead not far away. A slight shudder. perhaps combined with a kick from the back legs before dashing away, suggests a hit in the liver. It should also be found dead a short distance away.

If it jumps up with its head held low, then hunches up and moves off slowly, you can be equally certain that you have hit it in the stomach. Sometimes you can hear the sound of a hollow thud as the bullet strikes. This is one time when you can shoot at a moving deer with a clear conscience – if you manage a second, better placed bullet, you will save yourself a great deal of searching. If you cannot see if the animal has fallen, you will do well to wait ten minutes or so before moving forward to look for further signs. A deer with a stomach wound will often lie down as soon as it is in cover, and the sight of you may move it on before it has a chance to stiffen up.

A deer that goes down and struggles violently or manages to stand up again has probably been creased. A quick second shot is in order. To see a deer make off limping, perhaps in a curved run, is a more worrying sign of a broken leg. If you have the chance, shoot again even if it moving as a deer can go a long way in this condition and, even with the services of a good tracking dog, you may have a great deal of trouble finding it again.

Don't be put off by this list. As I said at the start, most muntjac will drop to the shot is fairly hit in a vital area. However, you should be alert to the signs if your target does make off, and when you move forward to where it was standing what you find there will help you to confirm the impression.

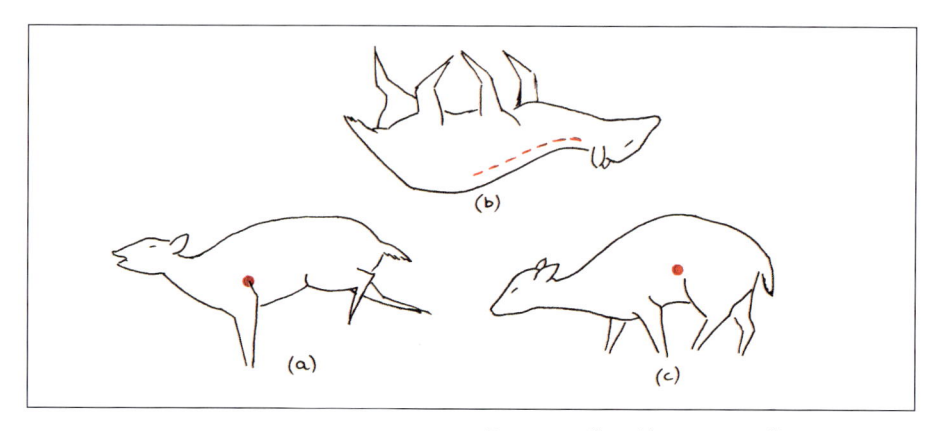

Reactions to Shot: (a) Heart/Lung (b) Crease (c) Gut)

The Follow-Up
Before you do anything else, make a careful note of your firing point in case you need to go back to it and retrace your steps.

If you can see the animal lying where it was shot, it is unlikely that you will have a problem. You should, however, always treat the animal as though it may still have traces of life in it until you have proved that it is dead. Approach it cautiously, ready to shoot if it starts to struggle or gets to its feet. Try to ensure that you always have a backstop for the bullet if this happens - a downhill approach, if available, is often best. If the animal is still moving, a second shot is the most humane way to finish it off. Fancy knife work is not recommended – remember that a muntjac buck in extremis can still do a lot of damage with his canines, and that the flailing hooves of any deer are sharp. Always remember to allow for the fact that the bullet will go a couple of inches low at point blank range. Touch the eyeball with the end of your stick - if there is no reaction, the animal is dead and you can move on to the gralloch.

Always assume that your target is still alive until you have proved otherwise. As you approach, be ready to fire again if it starts to struggle.

Alternately, the shot has been taken and the animal has disappeared. You may not be able to see if it has fallen where it stood, or it may have run on. If you have observed a reaction to the shot, you may have a good idea of what to expect but work on the principle that you may have to follow the animal up. At the very least stay where you are for five minutes (in less politically-correct days I would have advised long enough to smoke a cigarette) before moving in cautiously, ready for a second shot at all times. With luck, all will be well and you will find the animal lying there.

If the animal is not where you expect it to be you are going to have to follow it up. Always assume that you have hit it, even if you can find no sign. The odds are that it is not far away and your task is now to recover the carcase before it can spoil, or more importantly put the beast out of its misery if it is still alive and wounded.

Take your time and carefully examine the spot where you thought the animal was standing when it was hit for signs of blood and hair ('paint and pins' in the old language of stalking). In snow and frost they are quite obvious; sometimes they are surprisingly difficult to spot against normal vegetation. Get down on your hands and knees if necessary and run your hands across the ground to pick up any smears that might be there. Once you've found the start of the blood trail, mark it with something so that you can find it again easily. This is where some tissue paper, carried as part of your normal stalking kit, comes in handy. You can use more of the same to mark the blood trail as you follow it.

Once you have found the start of a blood trail, a close look at what is there will give you an indication of where you hit the animal. Bright red arterial blood is the best possible sign, indicating a heart shot. Equally encouraging is pink, frothy blood, perhaps with some pink lung tissue, indicating lungs. Both are good signs of mortal wounds – the animal is most likely lying dead very close by, and is likely to have run in a fairly straight line before collapsing.

Darker, browner blood and tissue is the sign of a liver wound – also fatal, though the animal might take a few minutes to expire although this might take a short time and it is best left for fifteen minutes or so before following up.

Bright red arterial blood is a good sign of a mortal wound. The animal should be lying dead close by.

You will most likely find it dead. Green stomach material indicates a gut shot. In such a case the animal might travel some distance before settling if disturbed again – at the moment it is probably close by, and is best left to stiffen up for at least half an hour, preferably twice as long, lest you, blundering in, terrify it into one last burst of effort to get away. If you give it a suitable 'soak time' you are more likely to find it dead, or at least less liable to move on before you can shoot again.

Hair and bone fragments, with little or no blood, are the worst possible sign of a broken leg. A deer can go a long way on three legs, and the wound is unlikely to be mortal. All that you can do is follow it up immediately, preferably with the aid of a good dog, and hope to get the chance of another shot. If nothing vital is touched by the bullet, a deer can recover from the most horrifying flesh wounds; blood is a medium red and the trail will peter out after a short while.

If a blood trail disappears quickly, you have two options left to you. The best is to enlist the services of a trained dog or, if one is not available, start casting left and right of the line that you have followed until you hopefully come across the dead animal. If you have marked the trail with tissue paper, the line will be obvious when you look behind you. In case it is not dead, your movements have to be slow and cautious with repeated scanning using the binoculars. Go as far as you think that the animal might have gone, and then as far again.

Do not give up until you have exhausted all efforts to find the animal. If you fail, do not try to hide the fact. Everyone makes mistakes occasionally, and it is better to admit to them than have others find them out. If you alert any other land users such as fellow stalkers, the local farmer or gamekeeper that there might be a wounded deer on the ground, it greatly increases your chances of recovering it.

Finally, always take care not to spoil the trail for a dog if you are going to use one to help you. Trampling over the trail just makes it more difficult to find the scent. By keeping to one side of it, you are leaving useful traces for the dog to follow. If the trail runs out, be careful not to disturb it where it continues beyond the ability of your limited senses to follow. A dog will inevitably smell what you cannot.

Use of Dogs
Every stalker should own, or at least have access to, a dog that is capable of tracking an animal that has been shot at and cannot be found. Training dogs for deer work is enough of a subject to fill a book in its own right, and has been covered by people far more capable of it than myself in other publications. However, a few brief notes on the value of a canine stalking companion are certainly in order at this point.

A dog that will follow a blood trail is an invaluable asset to any stalker.

Any dog with a nose can be trained to follow up a wounded deer, and can save you hours of searching, not to mention a wasted carcase if it is not found, or found too late to be rendered fit for human consumption. There are indeed breeds of dog that are ideally suited to the purpose, such as the HPR (hunting, pointing and retrieving) breeds, and the German teckel (a variety of dachshund) is, for its size, a tenacious and talented tracker. Any of the gundog breeds can be excellent, too, but do not discount the 'Heinz 57' mutt who is quite capable of demonstrating a talent given a little encouragement and training. It's surprising how quickly a dog learns the difference between game shooting and stalking – my ancient spaniel still gets wildly excited when he sees a shotgun, but is more sedately enthusiastic at the sight of a rifle case!

There are techniques, largely developed on the Continent, which can range from teaching the dog to bark at a found deer (some dogs will of course do this quite naturally without any need for special training) to use of the bringsel, a piece of wood or a strap attached to the collar which the dog is taught to take into its mouth to show its handler that it has found a dead deer. Such training is possible, but often long and involved. From a novice's point of view, basically encouraging a dog to follow the trail of a wounded animal is sufficient and can be built up through a simple process of familiarisation with what is required.

A dog's sense of smell is infinitely superior to a human's, and wherever possible the dog should be allowed the first crack at a scent trail. Deer can often do surprising things when wounded lightly enough to run, and the dog will smell what you can't see. No matter if you think that the dog is going off in the wrong direction, allow it to carry on. If it is used to the idea of tracking deer, it's more likely to be right than you are. If you do not have a dog with you and intend to call in someone to assist, do take care not to ruin a scent trail by blundering across it. The moment you decide that there is insufficient blood trail for you to follow up an animal on your own, you should mark the spot and leave any further tracking until the dog and its handler arrive. For this reason it makes sense to get into the habit of doing any visual tracking from a foot or two to one side of the blood trail itself.

If your dog is steady enough, it can become an invaluable companion on stalking expeditions rather than just being confined to the car as an 'insurance policy' against being needed for a follow up. It must be at your side where you can see it, and certainly not casting around you. Some dogs simply are not suited to this and do not have the patience for the sort of painstaking movement involved in stalking, but most get the idea quickly enough. Any intelligent dog will quickly come to understand what you are looking for. In time it will start to indicate deer that it has scented up-wind of you and will add to your success rates considerably. You will be amazed at how often you would simply have walked past a deer had it not been shown to you. When it comes to taking the shot, the dog must of course not be gun shy, and needs to learn that when the rifle comes up it needs to be behind, not in front of you, when you shoot or its hearing will be damaged.

Opinions vary as to the wisdom of encouraging your dog to pull down a wounded muntjac. Although even a dog as small as a spaniel is capable of immobilising a wounded deer up to the size of a roe until you are able to administer the *coup de grace*, you should be ever-mindful of the damage that a muntjac buck can inflict with his canines. If you are unfortunate enough to wound an immature or female muntjac, and your dog can be trusted to do the job properly, I do not believe that you need to hold back from sending it in. But I would urge you to think twice before committing it to the pursuit of a lightly-wounded buck. I have known some horrific cases of dogs which have required urgent veterinary attention involving multiple stitches after such encounters.

A very experienced deer dog with scars resulting from an encounter with a muntjac buck. You must be very confident in your dog's abilities before committing it to the pursuit of a lightly wounded animal.

This spaniel received extensive wounds to its back and side from a young muntjac buck, resulting in some 35 stitches

Safety

I make no apologies for ending this chapter with a note on safety. Stalking means shooting, and any shooting that is not done with a mind to where the bullet will end up is liable to be dangerous. Before you take off the safety catch you must be absolutely sure of where the bullet is going to end its journey. Never, never rely on it staying in the body of your target deer - 99 times out of 100 it will carry on and be capable of killing whatever else it hits for a very long distance.

Neither should you rely on screens of trees or undergrowth to break a bullet up. The only safe recipient for a bullet is a good solid earth backstop. It's easy to forget in the heat of the moment. Responsible shooting is always safe; thoughtlessness can lead to tragedy.

CHAPTER 7
Carcase Handling and Preparation

Congratulations – you've located the shot animal and confirmed that it is dead. Now the work begins. What follows must ensure that the carcase is speedily and hygienically processed to ensure that it can enter the human food chain safely. While you are doing this you need to keep your eyes open for anything unusual – more of which in the next chapter. Whether the carcase is destined for a game dealer or your own household, it is your responsibility to ensure that it is kept clean, uncontaminated, and fit for the purpose.

The Gralloch
In an ideal world, the gralloch needs to take place within about twenty to thirty minutes of death. After this time the build up of gases within the stomach causes ballooning, and there is an increased danger of the carcase being tainted. After a few hours (especially under warm summer conditions) the meat may well end up unfit for human consumption.

Prepare the site carefully. Make sure that you are aware from prying eyes, as the average user of a public footpath may not be that impressed to find you. If necessary, move the carcase to somewhere less public, and where the inevitable gore that you leave behind you will not be easily stumbled upon. To the casual eye, the bloody aftermath of a gralloch may look as though murder most foul has been committed.

Before you start, make sure that you unload your rifle. I always find it useful to lay my jacket (outside downwards) flat on the ground and pile my equipment (binoculars, gloves, face veil etc) on top of it so that nothing is forgotten afterwards. Then make sure that what you need is easily to hand, as it is not helpful to go rummaging in pockets for plastic bags or spare latex gloves when your hands are already covered in blood. Some may question the need to wear gloves when gralloching. I suggest that not only do they save you hunting around for a water supply to clean up afterwards, but they also give you a bit of piece of mind. Although muntjac are remarkably healthy animals by and large, you never know what you are going to come across when you open one up so it helps to play safe.

Give some consideration to getting the animal away from contact with the ground while you gralloch. This will not only make the job easier for you, but it will also reduce the potential for carcase contamination. A lightweight plastic groundsheet is a good start, or actually hanging the carcase from a suitable tree by the hind legs will make things considerably easier once you have completed work on the front and back ends and are ready to move to the middle. A couple of 'S' hooks weigh next to nothing and can be carried in the pocket or backpack for the purpose.

There's no need to worry about 'bleeding' the carcase. This procedure is used for the larger species of deer, especially when they are 'field gralloched' and left with the heart and lungs in place while they are removed from the open hill. There is no need for this with muntjac, and the hydraulic shock of a modern high velocity bullet anywhere forward of the diaphragm does the job in any case.

There are any number of variations on how the gralloch can be performed, including sawing the breastbone through and opening up the pelvic girdle. The following method has the advantage of being simple to perform, while exposing the least areas to potential contamination or meal spoilage:

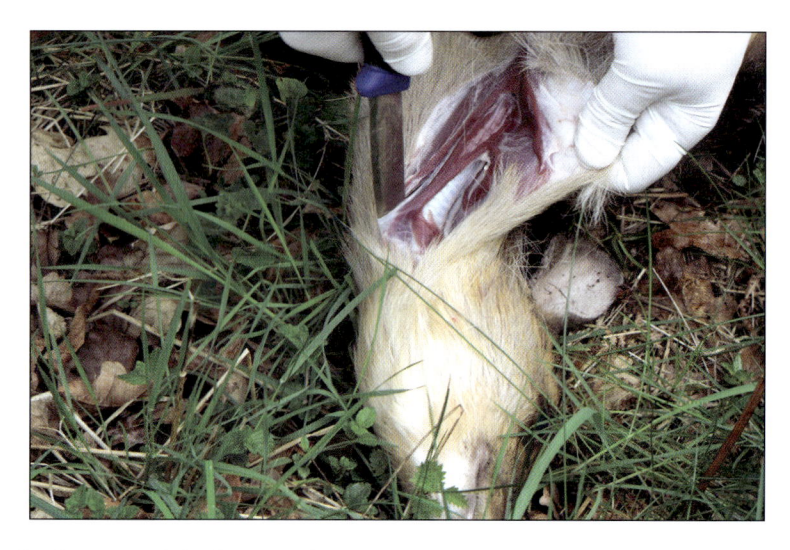

With the animal laid on its back, slit open the throat from breastbone to under the chin. Work your fingers behind the windpipe to separate it from the neck and cut it as close to the head as possible.

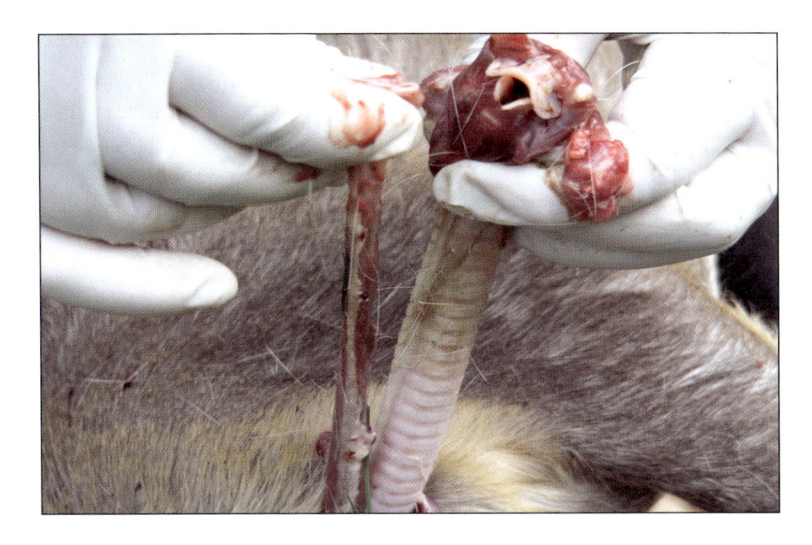

Separate the gullet, which runs up the back of the windpipe. Scrape the flesh from it using your knife blade held at right angles. Tie a knot in the gullet to stop undigested plant material coming back through it when you eventually pull if free.

Now move to the back end of the carcase. Cut carefully around the vent and, with a combination of small cuts and working the tissue free with your fingers, separate all contents from the pelvic cavity taking care not to puncture the bladder. You will be grateful for a knife with a small blade at this point. You may find it helpful to clamp a hind leg behind your knee to raise up the rump and allow easier access whilst you are doing this.

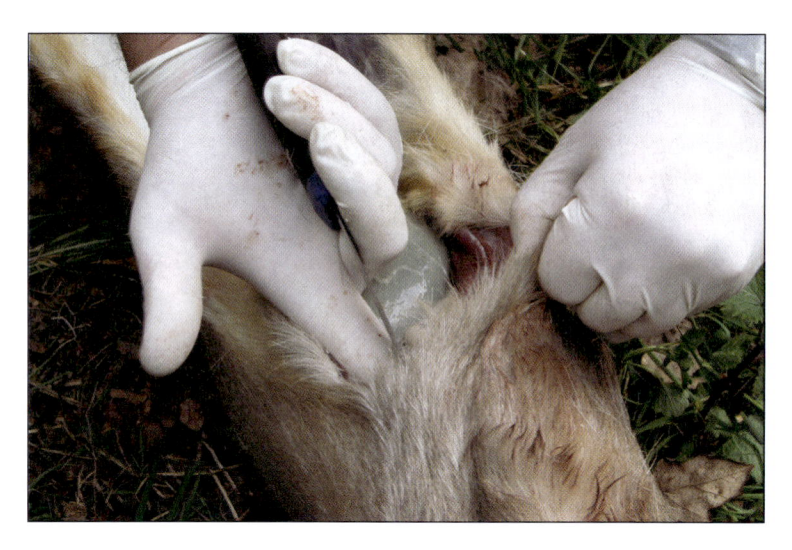

Now, with the carcase lying on its back or hanging at a convenient height, make a careful cut in the skin covering the stomach, holding the knife at a very shallow angle to avoid puncturing the stomach itself. As soon as you have made a small opening, insert two fingers and use them to lift the skin away from the body cavity contents while you continue the cut as far as the breastbone and back to the pelvis. Cut away the udder (does) or sexual organs (bucks) at this point.

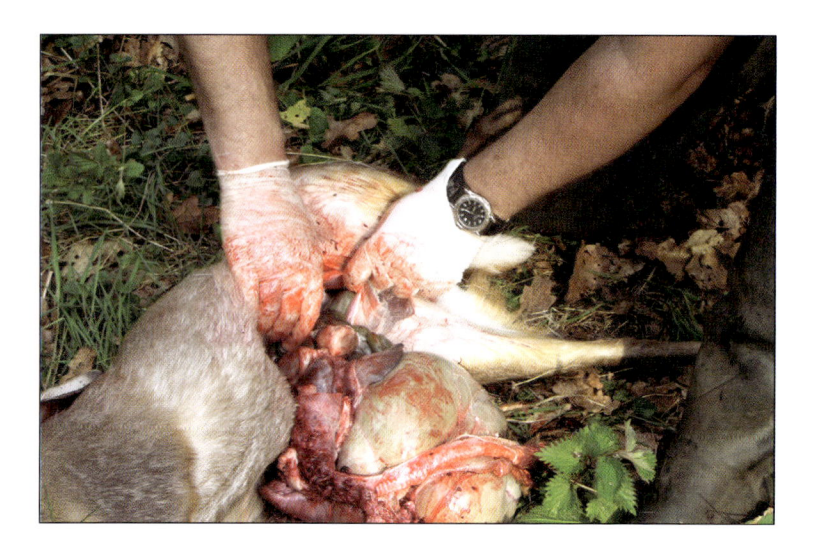

Gently pull the vent and rear body contents free of the carcase, using a minimum of knife work and working your fingers behind them to free them where necessary instead.

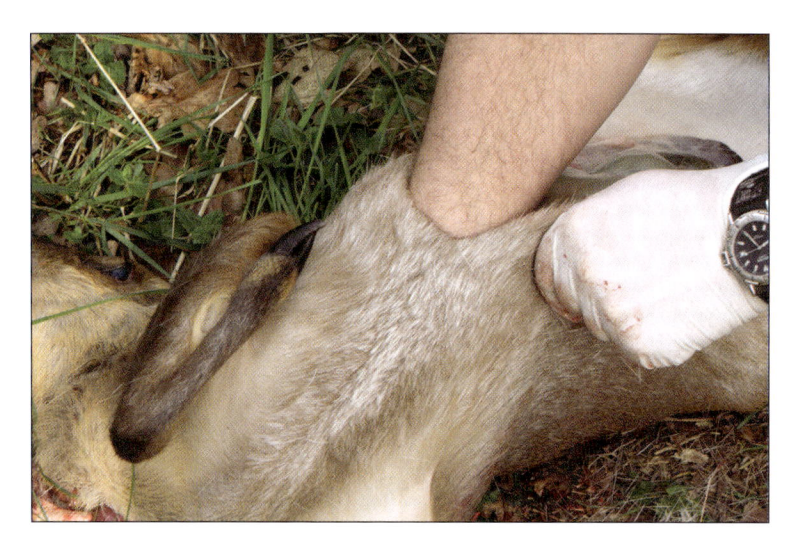

Cut around the diaphragm and use your hands to free the heart, lungs and windpipe from the body cavity (there should be no need for knife work if you do this carefully). Take special care not to cut yourself on any ribs that might have been smashed by the bullet on its way through. Taking a grip as far forward as you can on the windpipe, pull the organs free of the body cavity. Free any parts that are attached to the back of the animal with a knife if necessary.

Empty the body cavity by holding up the back legs and draining any remaining blood out. Try to avoid getting any blood on the haunches or in the general area of the pelvis. Hanging the carcase by the hind legs assists further drainage.

With practice, a gralloch is the work of a few minutes and will leave a clean, healthy carcase ready to hang in the larder. If the shot has gone too far back in the body, or perhaps come off a rib at a strange angle, you will need to clean up the carcase interior as best you can to prevent the green stomach contents from contaminating it.

Slit between the tendon and bone at the heel of each hind leg to hang the carcase using a stick. The lower leg will eventually be discarded anyway and there is no risk of meat contamination. Clean lardering equipment (a gambrel or S hooks) should be used when 'hocking' at the more usual point behind the knee.

Now is the time to separate and bag up the liver and kidneys for your own use (it is no accident that you never find deer liver in a butchers – it is the 'stalkers perks' and far superior to any lamb or calf's liver). A fresh muntjac liver, sliced and coated in flour before being fried in butter, is a breakfast fit for the hungriest stalker. If you don't eat the heart, which is delicious minced, consider taking it back to boil up with the lungs for dog food. You might also consider emptying the stomach of its contents for tripes. If the animal is going to your local game dealer, you need to check whether he will require the heart, lungs, liver and spleen which are a pre-requisite for examination if the carcase is going into the export market.

What is left, namely the stomach and intestines, needs to be disposed of discreetly once you have checked the lymph glands for any sign of abnormality. Suitable alternatives are burying it, or pushing down a convenient rabbit hole and kicking the entrance in (with, I hope, a muttered apology to the rabbits). What you must take care over is that it is not discovered by dog walkers and the like – even the most pampered poodle would be unlikely to pass up such a wonderful opportunity!

Before you leave with your prize, don't forget to check that you have picked up your knife.

Carcase Extraction & Storage
The muntjac stalker is fortunate in having such an easily portable quarry, so don't spoil all your careful work producing a clean carcase by dragging it off to the car. Now is the time to get it into the backpack or carrying sling and keep it off the ground. If you have neither, you can either tie all four legs together to make a temporary sling or hock the back legs with your stick to make a shoulder support – both methods are good for only a short distance, mind, before they get very uncomfortable.

You should have a suitable container in the car to take the carcase. Anything that is waterproof and easily cleaned out will do. A trip to the local DIY store will produce the sort of box that toys are kept in. These usually come with a lid which is handy to conceal the contents from prying eyes when you are travelling or transporting the contents from car to game larder. You should obviously not transport your dog alongside the carcase for food hygiene reasons.

A purpose-made tray for transporting deer carcases. The grid at the bottom allows air to circulate and blood to drain away from the carcase.

A muslin tube will protect the carcase from flies in warm weather

Where are you going to hang the carcase? Out of sight of neighbours or passers-by, clearly, is a must. Anywhere that is cool and well ventilated will do, and for most of us this means a garage or garden shed. It also needs to be fly-proof, and a purpose built game larder large enough to accommodate two or three animals is a good idea if you are doing a lot of stalking. Failing that, a nylon or muslin net can be used to cover it. If you leave any meat exposed it takes no time at all before the flies find it and clusters of eggs appear. Many stalkers use chiller cabinets of the sort that you find in shops selling soft drinks etc. Once the shelves have been removed and a hanging bar added, a small one will store a couple of carcasses and is especially useful in the heat of summer. It will take up very little space in the corner of a garage and need only be switched on when you require it.

This is a good time to remove the head and legs for several reasons (before you do so, you should weigh the animal for your records). Firstly, it is less like a dead Bambi if someone inadvertently looks in and sees it. Secondly, it is easier to store. Finally, this is normally how a game dealer will want to receive it (they don't like paying for any parts that they can't use!). To remove the head, make a cut immediately behind the ears and continue either side of the head to the base of the chin. When you have severed all meat and muscle down to the bone, simply grasp the chin in one hand and the top of the head with the other and twist the head in a circle at right angles to the body. When you feel the vertebrae give, work your knife into the gap to complete the job.

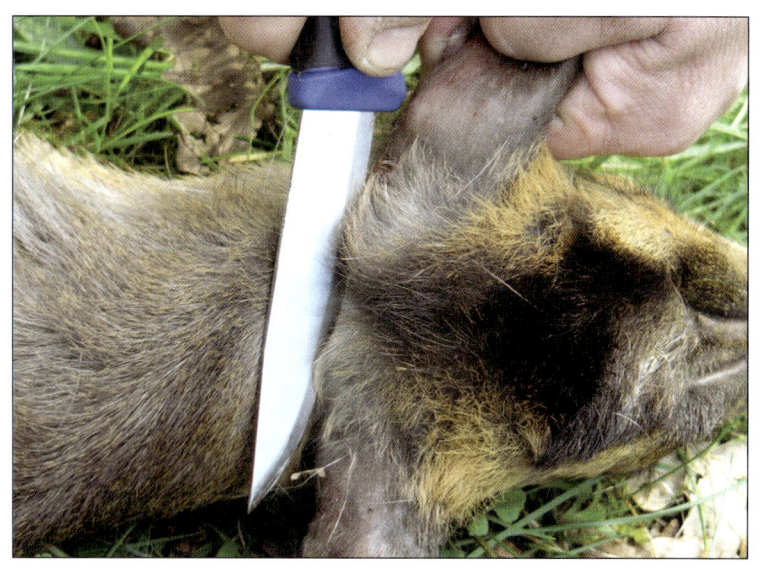

Take care severing the legs, particularly the hind ones, for if you cut too high there will be no support from behind the leg sinews to hang the animal. There are two knee joints on the hind leg, and the lower one (the one that you want to cut) is further down the leg than you might expect. If you run the knife blade down the front of the leg you will feel both as notches in the bone. Cut through the front of the bottom one and continue the cut all the way round the leg. Twist it at right angles to the upper leg and it should part easily. Again, finish the cut with the knife.

All that remains now is to hang it up using a gambrel or a couple of S hooks. A spreader bar (made of washable metal or plastic) will help to hold the body cavity open, which will assist in faster cooling of the carcase. The quicker this happens, the better the meat quality will eventually be. If necessary, wipe the inside of the body cavity clean of blood and any other material which might taint the meat with dry kitchen towels. Occasionally a carcase will be messier, and may call for a damp cloth. Whatever you do, don't leave it wet, as mould will quickly form.

When removing the lower legs, take care not to make the cut too high up.

Some simple lardering equipment: gambrel and S hooks, scales and bone shears

The Roesafe is an ingenious fly-proof larder that folds flat when not in use. It easily accommodates at least three muntjac carcases.

A chiller is an excellent solution to hanging carcases in hot weather. This one will hold up to seven muntjac, and was purchased second-hand for next to nothing. For the average stalker, something a fraction of the size that will hold two or three carcases is more than adequate.

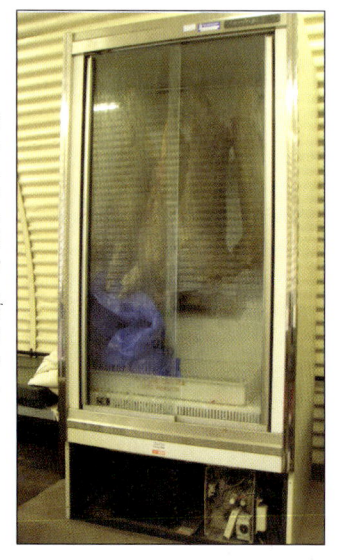

How long you hang the carcase for before moving on to skinning and jointing it is very much up to you. As *rigor mortis* sets in quickly after death and drops out again some 36 hours later, this should be regarded as the bare minimum. In warm weather you don't want to leave it much longer or the meat will quickly go off. Even in winter, I tend not to hang a muntjac carcase for longer than four or five days anyway as the venison simply doesn't need improving in the same way that some other species of deer benefit from hanging. These periods can be extended if you are keeping the carcase in a chiller, and your nose will tell you very quickly if the meat is on the turn! Alternatively, compare the 'give' in the flesh of the haunch with a finger tip with that of your cheek. If the consistency of both is about the time, it's time to get convert the carcase into a more cook-friendly form.

From Larder to Kitchen (Basic Butchery)
The carcase is always best left in the skin until you are ready to butcher it, otherwise the meat exposed to the air will go hard very quickly. Skinning a muntjac is very straightforward but if you are more used to the likes of roe you will find it a little more time-consuming. The skin comes away from the meat of the latter quite easily and you can use your fingers and knuckles to separate the two. In the case of the muntjac, the skin is much more firmly attached to the meat (especially around the rump area) and you will find that a bit more careful knife work is required.

On the other hand, the butchery of a muntjac carcase couldn't be simpler because of the size of the animal involved. There are three basic cuts - the saddle, haunches and shoulders - and whatever else is salvaged becomes stewing meat or mince. Unless you are into fancy butchery, forget anything more complicated. Even on a large animal, the shoulders do not carry a great deal of meat and many people simply bone them. By the time a bullet has done its work, a good deal of the front end of the carcase may only be fit for the dog pot anyway.

Before you start, lay out your equipment. You will obviously need a sharp skinning knife - a spare one is also useful as skinning blunts a blade very quickly. A bin bag should be ready to receive anything you want to dispose of. A tray covered with a second bin bag is useful to lay the joints on, as is a bowl to take any off-cuts, and a bone saw makes light work of any heavy cutting that you will need to do. If you have a dog, a large pot will take any meat spoilt by the bullet and bones for boiling. Latex gloves and a damp cloth for wiping any stray hairs away are also handy.

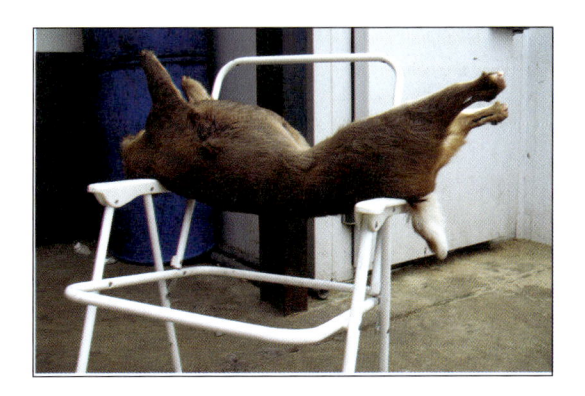

A folding deck chair frame makes a very useful trestle to assist skinning.

First you have to skin the carcase. If you have a trestle, you may find it easier to lay the carcase on its back and complete work on the underside before hanging the animal up and continuing. Assuming that you are going to start with the animal hanging by its hind legs (using two separate S hooks, as a single gambrel will swing about too much), the following sequence illustrates what needs to be done:

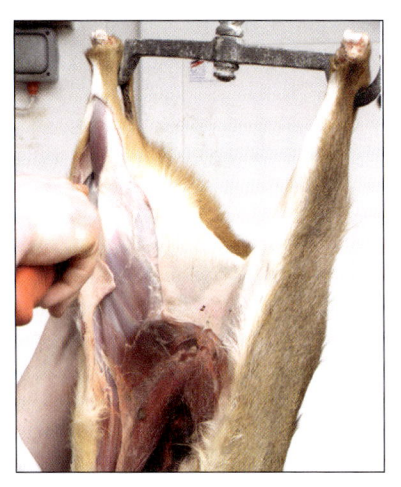

Start with a cut up the inside of both hind legs and separate the skin from the flesh all the way around each, using your fingers where you can and a knife where necessary. If you pull the skin away from the meat and cut carefully with the blade almost flat against it you will find that you do not cut into the meat. Try to use the knife tip rather than the broad edge of the blade.

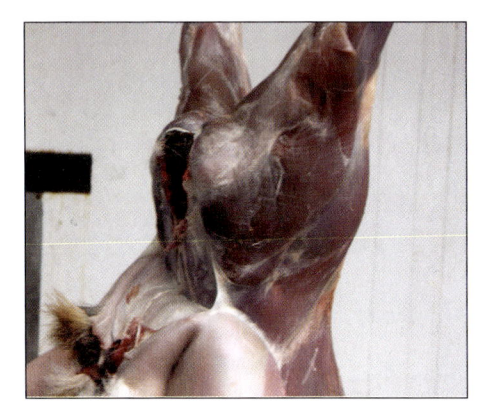

Once you have worked the skin off as far as the tail, cut off the latter as close to the rump as possible. If you lay the knife blade against the top of it and press down you will find that it separates easily. Carry on separating the skin from the back and sides, working downwards. Take care to keep the outside of the skin away from the flesh you expose, otherwise you will end up with a carcase covered with hairs.

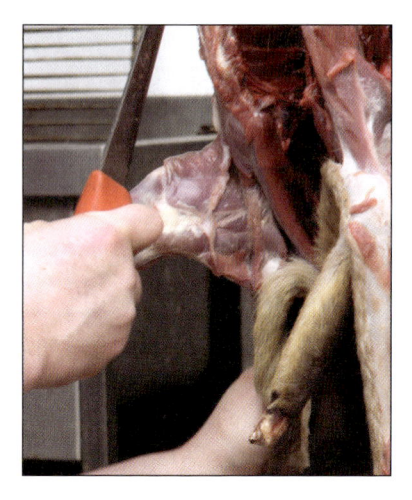

Cut up the inside of each foreleg and free the skin from around them (you will find that this part of the process is much easier if you have done it on a trestle before hanging the carcase up.

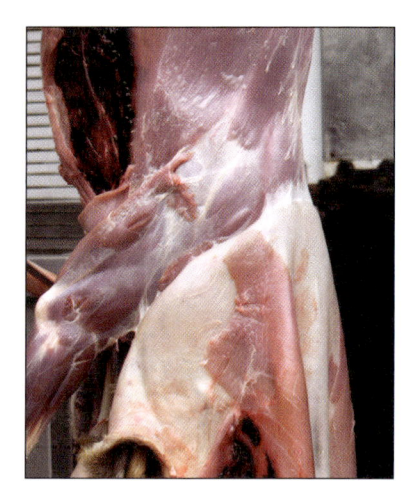

Carry on removing the skin until you reach the end of the neck. If you do not want to keep the skin for tanning, lay it outside-down on the floor to wrap up any discarded sharp bones later on (this stops them from puncturing any bag you put them into for disposal). And there you have it - a clean carcase ready for jointing.

Now it's time to move on to the jointing. A change of gloves is a good idea at this point. If you are not wearing any, you should wash your hands and at the same time ensure that your knives are clean. With the carcase hanging by the hind legs, you worked from top to bottom whilst skinning. Now you will joint it working from bottom to top.

Remove each foreleg by lifting it away from the body and cutting the connecting muscle behind. Note that this is all that connects the shoulder to the body.

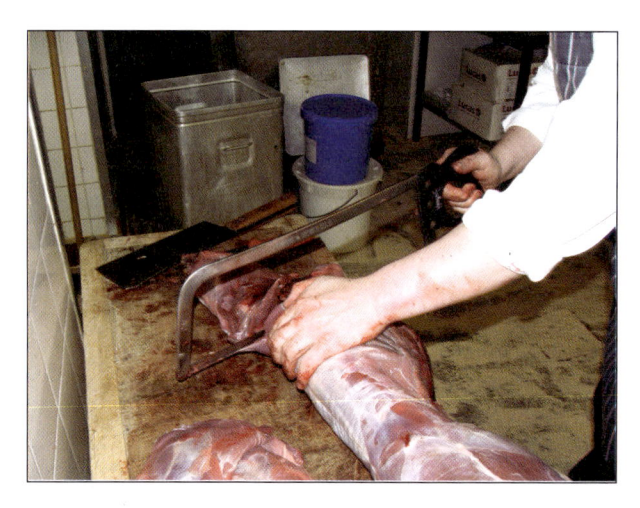

Decide where the saddle is to begin and mark the point with a light cut. This should be about two ribs in towards the neck end counting from the saddle. Either remove all useable meat from below this point while the carcase is still hanging, or cut the entire front section away on a clean, flat surface if you have one available. If the ribs are not too badly damaged by the bullet strike, they can be cut off with the bone saw and saved for hot pots or spare ribs (although there is not much meat to be had on them).

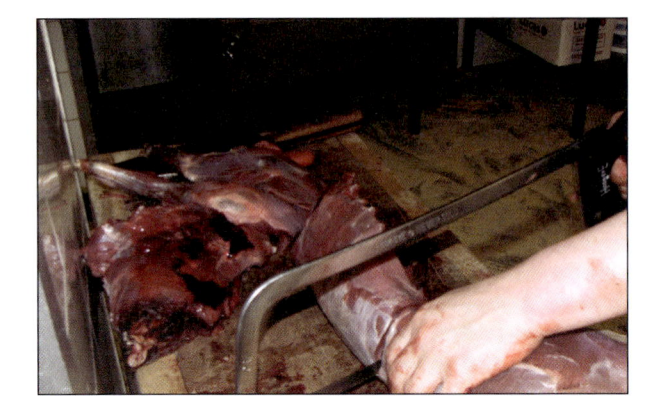

Once you have removed as much meat as you can from the front end of the carcase, cut it away from the start of the saddle with the bone saw and wrap it in the skin before bagging it for disposal. Then cut the back of the saddle away just in front of the haunches, using a knife to start with then taking a bone saw to complete the job. Alternately, you can do a neater job and avoid wasting meat by making a backwards cut at 45 degrees along the inside of each haunch bone to where the last vertebra joins the pelvic bone; the whole saddle should then lift away with a little help from the knife.

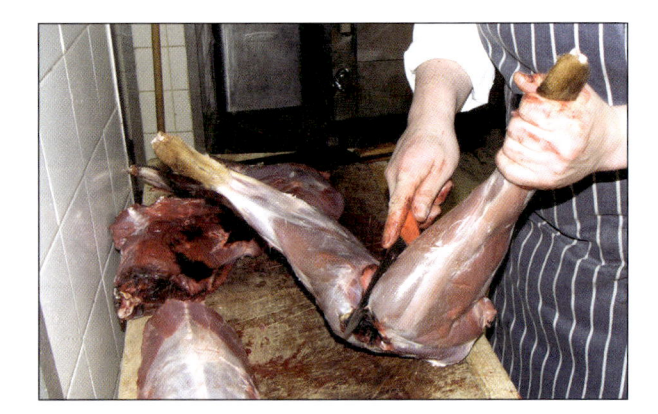

To finish the job, simply cut straight down the pelvic girdle with the bone saw to separate the haunches. If you wish, you can take the pelvic girdle away completely with some deft knife work, and remove the lower leg at the knee for stewing (there is very little meat below this point anyway).

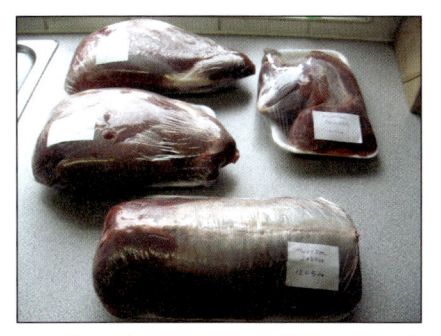

A saddle, two haunches and a shoulder wrapped and labelled ready for the freezer

A mincer makes short work of off-cuts of venison, and allows the cook extra versatility.

This is the most basic method of butchering. There are plenty of refinements on it – you can, for instance, make chops of the front end (which will be small but tasty) or larger 'double' Barnsley chops from the saddle. Do take care with cooking these though, as venison is much leaner than lamb and dries out very quickly when grilled.

You will probably be surprised at how small such a large carcase has become once broken down. All that's left now is to present the meat to the cook in a way that keeps things happy in the kitchen. Use a damp cloth to wipe away any traces of blood or hair. Joints and saddles can be wrapped in clingfilm for freezing, while smaller cuts can be bagged. If you are producing mince, I have found it best to wrap 1/2lb portions in clingfilm and then freeze them in a larger plastic bag. A cheap mincer is a very useful buy from any kitchenware shop, and muntjac mince is versatile – you can use it in just about any recipe that calls for beef mince.

Don't forget to label everything with what it is and the date, before it goes to join the mystery objects that seem to lurk at the bottom of every freezer.

Trophy Preparation

Although most of us are not trophy hunters, you will occasionally shoot a special head that you may wish to keep. A clean, well-mounted trophy is a fitting memento of a special occasion, not simply a 'didn't I do well' hanging on the wall. It is not difficult to do the job properly and well worth the effort involved.

The tools that you need to hand are a sharp knife, wood saw, long-nosed pliers, a boiling pot large enough to contain the head and a shallow dish (glass or other easily washed material). In addition you will need a few crystals of washing soda, a bottle of hydrogen peroxide (as strong a solution as you can get at the chemists, normally 6% or 9%), and some cotton wool. There are any number of variations on how to prepare a trophy. The sequence below shows how to produce a 'long nose' cut, although you might prefer to leave the entire skull intact.

When you get the carcase home, remove the head and leave it to soak in a bucket of cold water. This will make it easier to skin when you get round to doing it. If you haven't got time, you can freeze it - but remember to wrap it well and warn other freezer users! Simply put it in a bucket of water to defrost the night before you plan to deal with it.

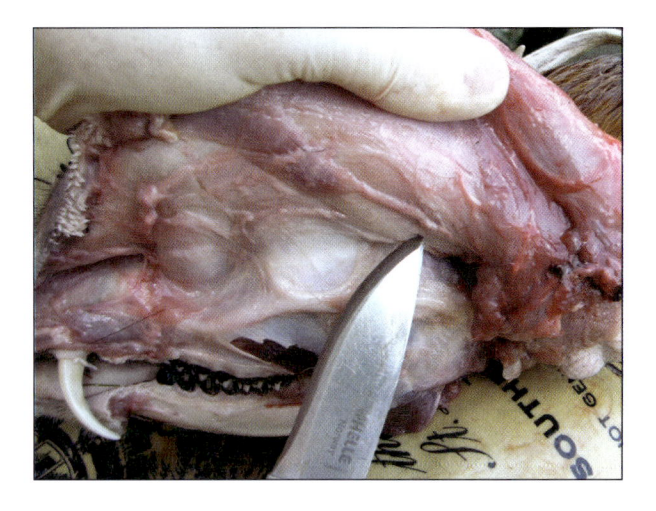

Remove all skin and as much flesh as possible from the head. Take special care not to score the surface of the skull, and when clearing out the areas of the sub-orbital glands where the bone is very thin and easy to puncture. Remove the tongue and sever the muscles around the lower jaw. This can now be removed by bending it backwards until it separates.

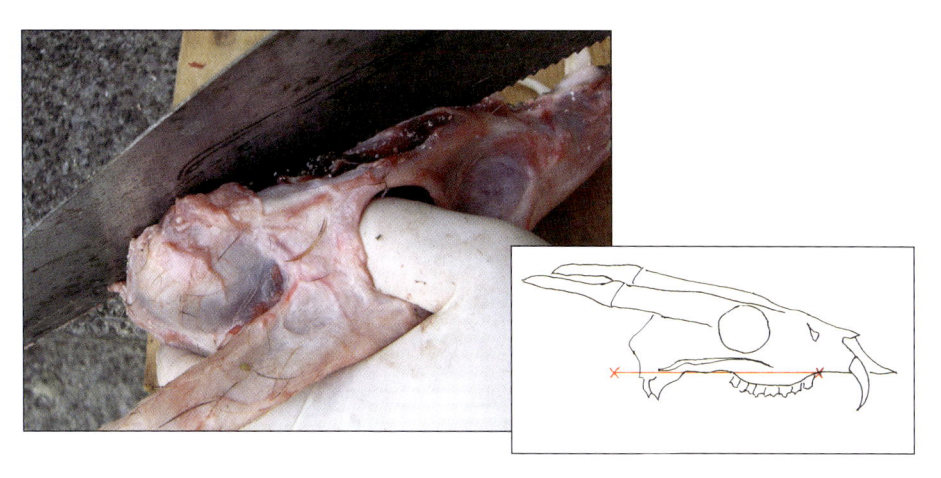

The skull should to be cut horizontally below the eye and sub-orbital gland sockets, removing the upper teeth but leaving the upper palate untouched and the canines and their sockets in place. Don't try to remove the canines, as this is virtually impossible at this stage and the bone around the sockets is fragile. You should also consider keeping at least one side of the lower jaw for your records and comparing for age with other animals you shoot.

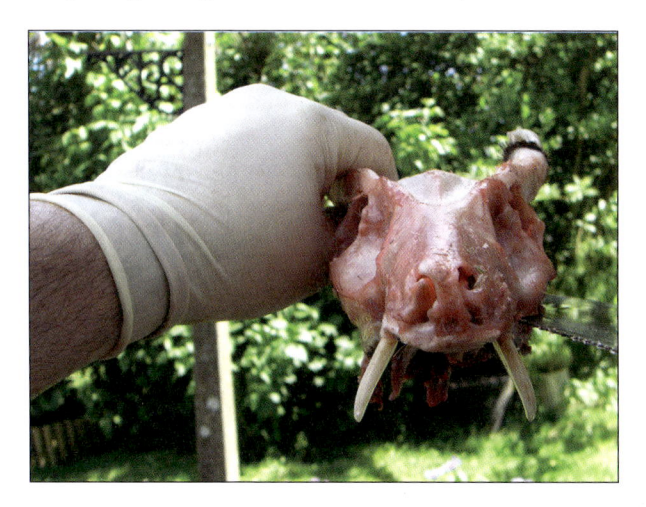

Saw carefully, stopping frequently to ensure that the blade is heading for the same point at the opposite side of the skull. Be careful not to chip or damage the canine teeth. If you find that you are going too far off line, simply stop sawing and start again at the other side. Don't worry if you end up slightly out, as any minor variations can be removed later with a power sander or file later if need be. Clear out the skull contents. If you have chosen to keep the skull intact, a piece of bent coat hanger is helpful.

Bring enough water to submerge the skull to the boil and add no more than half a teaspoon of washing soda (although not strictly essential, this will help to degrease the skull and make subsequent cleaning easier). Unless your household is particularly understanding, a gas burner in the garage or workshop is perhaps a more practical option to the kitchen as the smell is not to everyone's taste. Submerge the skull as far as the tops of the pedicles in the boiling water, taking care to keep the antlers themselves clear, and hold the skull in that position with a clamp or bent wire coathanger. Boil for about 45 minutes. Much longer, and the bone may start to soften and come apart (if it does, it's not the end of the world as it can be joined again with wood glue once completely dry).

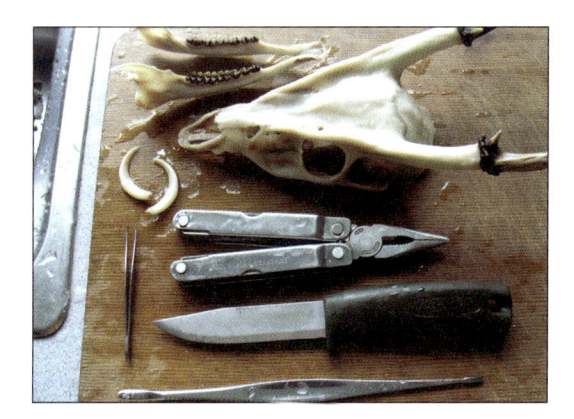

Remove from the water and clean all remaining flesh and tissue from the bone. Most will come away if scraped with a fingernail; a knife and pliers will take care of the rest. Take special care removing the cartilage and other matter from within the nose and behind the sub-orbital gland sockets, as the bone is very delicate in places. The thin tool at the bottom of the photograph was provided by a friendly dentist, and is excellent for this purpose. The canine teeth will have become loose, so remove them carefully and clean them off. Do not let the bone dry out at this stage or it will not bleach properly.

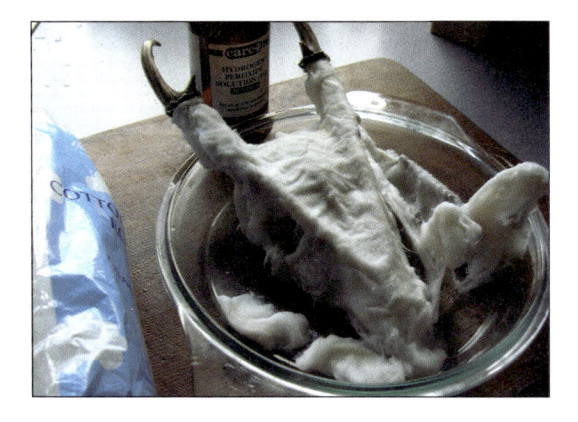

Once all tissue has been removed from the skull, cover all of the bone surfaces (inside and out) with a thin layer of cotton wool, tissue paper or muslin, taking care not to touch the antlers with it. Stand the whole thing in a shallow dish, add the canine teeth and the lower jaw if it is being kept, and pour the hydrogen peroxide onto the cotton wool. This will clean and bleach all that it comes into contact with, so don't get any on the antlers (if there is an accident, they can be touched up later with a solution of potassium permanganate or a little brown boot polish).

Leave for a few hours, or preferably overnight. Remove the cotton wool, rinse everything well under cold water and leave to dry at room temperature. The hydrogen peroxide can be squeezed out of the cotton wool (wear a latex glove) and returned to its bottle to be re-used - store it in a dark, cool place.

Once all is dry, sand the base of the skull level if the original saw cut was uneven and return the canine teeth to their sockets. If you can't remember which way to replace them, the shinier side faces inwards. A drop of superglue will hold them in place. Mount the whole thing on a suitable plaque using either a purpose-made clamp fitting (available from stalking suppliers) or a small piece of wood carved to a rough fit and fixed inside the skull cavity with wood glue (which dries clear). You can even use superglue to fix it to the plaque if you do not want to mess about with fittings. Make a note on the back of the plaque saying where and when the animal was shot and get the family's permission to hang it somewhere suitable. And there you are - a clean, odour free trophy that you can be proud of.

An alternative way or presenting your trophy; the same cut as the example, but mounted flat on a shield with the canines separate.

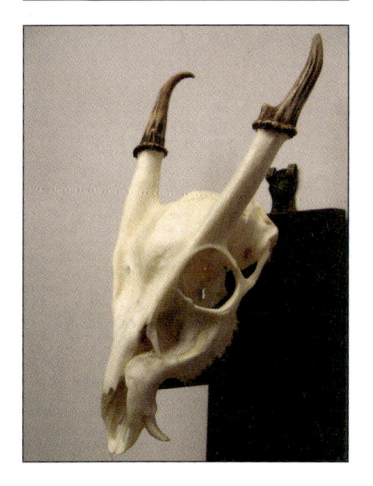

It is not necessary to cut at all – here the skull has been left intact and mounted at an angle

Muntjac – Managing an Alien Species

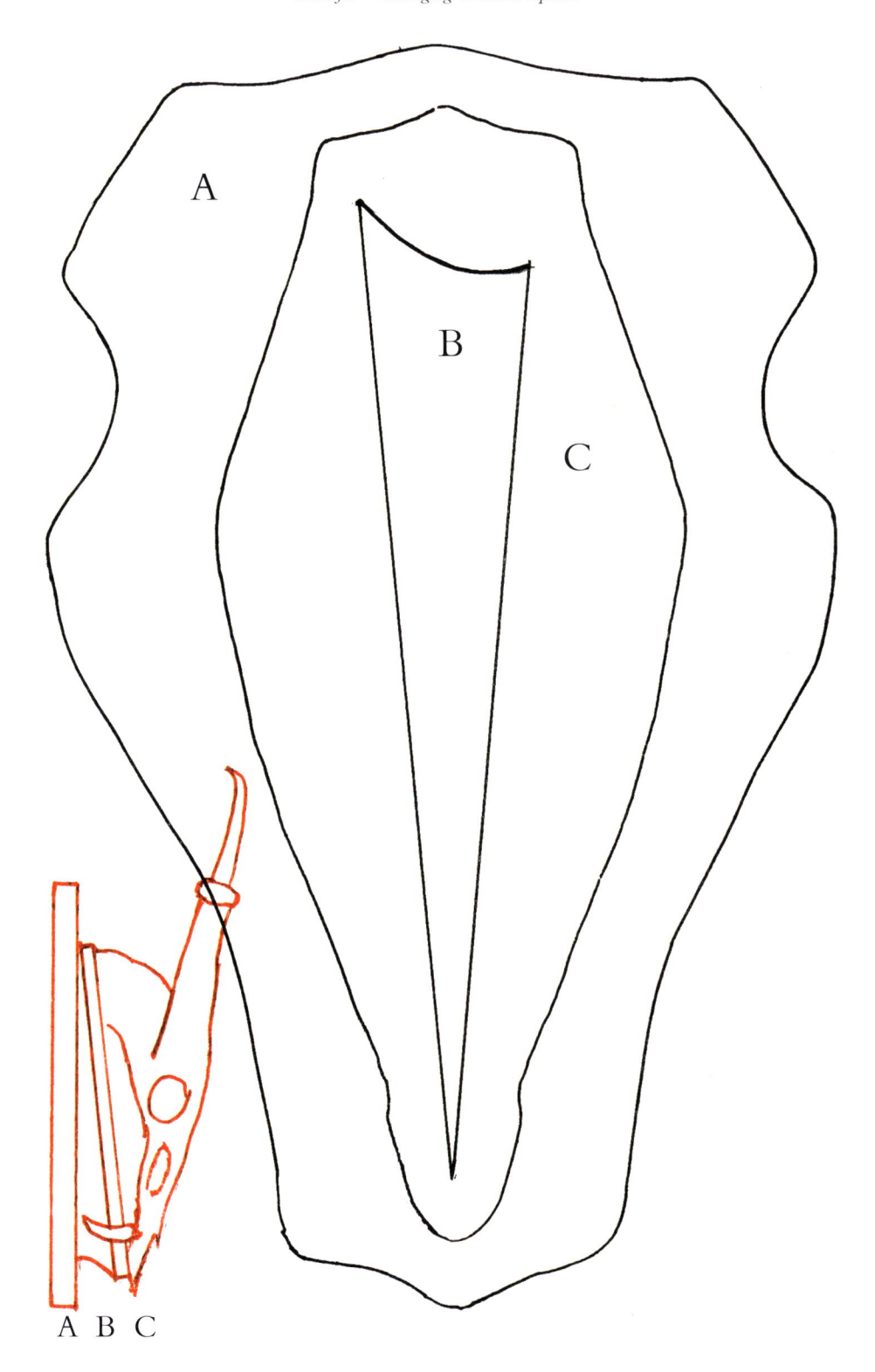

A

B

C

A B C

165

Trophy Measurement

If you believe that you have shot a buck with a particularly fine head, you may want to see if it qualifies for medal status under CIC (Conseil International de la Chasse) rules. An official measurer must assess it before a medal can be awarded; they frequently attend game fairs for this purpose or can be contacted through the British Deer Society. In the meantime, it is quite easy to apply the formula yourself first to see if your trophy comes close. Unlike other species of deer, there is no need for any weighing of the skull or immersing it in water to determine volume, and measurements can be taken equally successfully from a dead animal, a prepared skull or a fully mounted trophy.

All that you need is a tape measure (all measurements are taken in centimetres). First measure the inside span at the widest point between the two main beams (1). Then measure the main beams themselves along the outside of the antler, from the tip to the bottom edge of the coronet (2). Measure the brow tine (if present) along the lower side, from the upper edge of the coronet to the tip of the tine (3) – note that if the measurement is less than 1cm it will not count as a tine and cannot be scored. Finally, measure the circumference of each coronet (4) and the circumference of each beam at the mid-way point (5). If there is any difference in length between the left and right canines, whether a canine is broken or not, this also needs to be deducted from the final score. Use the table below to calculate the final score (an example measurement is shown in brackets).

SCORE DATA	A Span Credit (cm)	B Left (cm)	C Right (cm)	D Difference (cm)
1. Inside Span between Main Beams	(11.8)			
2. Length of main Beam		(10.5)	(10.2)	(0.3)
3. Length of Brow Tine		(1.2)	(1.6)	(0.4)
4. Circumference of Coronet		(7.9)	(8.1)	(0.2)
5. Circumference of antler at mid-distance up beam		(3.1)	(3.0)	(0.1)
6. COLUMN TOTALS	(11.8)	(22.7)	(22.9)	(1.0)
	Add A+B+C (57.4)	Subtract D (1.0)	FINAL SCORE (56.40 Bronze)	

Medal scores are: Gold 61 points or more.
　　　　　　　　　Silver between 58.5 and 60.9.
　　　　　　　　　Bronze 56 or above.

Muntjac – Managing an Alien Species

Measuring trophies at the CLA Game Fair. The formula for muntjac is less complicated than it is for other species, and can be applied to a head that has not been prepared in any way.

The top scoring UK muntjac head at the time of writing. It was shot in Gloucestershire in 1997 and achieved 79.5 points under CIC rules.

The UK second-best muntjac, shot in Hampshire in 2003 and measuring 78.3 points.

A short shoulder mount of excellent quality, ready for hanging

A superb full body mount by John Hopkins, seen here in use as part of a BDS Game Fair display.

Taxidermy

The head (or 'shoulder mount') of a good muntjac buck makes an excellent trophy, and there are plenty of good taxidermists out there who will be able to set it up for you. Beware choosing one without seeing his work first, as there are some real travesties out there that look more like badly stuffed teddy bears. It's worth collecting business cards at country fairs when you see work that you like, against the day that you actually shoot something that you want mounted. It will probably cost you a lot less than you expected as well, and the only challenge may be persuading the rest of your household that it is worthy of display!

You have to decide very quickly if you want the animal set up once you have shot it, as the means by which you gralloch it will vary greatly from the way you usually do it. The cut will have to be up the back of the neck rather than the front, this being the side that will not show, and the taxidermist will want as much skin from the shoulder area as possible if he is to do a worthwhile job. Skin to the top of the neck, but I'd advise leaving the head itself to the expert. Simply remove it from the top vertebra and put the whole lot into the deep freeze if necessary until you can get it to him.

With a muntjac you can also consider a whole body mount as it takes up very little space. The finished article is no bigger than the family dog and considerably cheaper to feed! This time the skinning cuts are up the insides of each leg, leaving the areas that will need to be joined again on the underside of the body. If you live close to your chosen taxidermist, he may prefer to do all of the skinning himself but it's always worth seeking his advice before you go ahead.

CHAPTER 8
Health and Disease

Deer in general are very healthy creatures, and muntjac in particular seem to be almost astonishingly so. Apart from the usual burdens of external parasites, it is extremely rare to find anything untoward in a muntjac carcase. However, the responsible stalker must be aware of what to look for and what action to take if he finds signs of anything unusual.

It's worth getting into the habit of checking a carcase from the moment that it is shot. Perhaps the deer was behaving abnormally in the first place – this in itself might offer clues that demand further attention. Then start with an external examination before commencing the gralloch, looking for anything out of the ordinary – growths, sores, old wounds and the like. Have a look inside the mouth, paying special attention to the tongue, to see if there are any unusual sores or other marks. Tooth wear will give you an idea of the animal's age. It is not unusual to find external parasites in small numbers. Keds move fast all over the body, but lice and ticks, more often found in the warmer areas, such as the groin, are more easily spotted. Large numbers of lice in particular may be an indication of over-population, while tick numbers tend to rise and fall with the seasons.

As the gralloch progresses check the internal organs for the unusual, and do not be afraid to seek advice if you are not sure. Treat any scars or discolouring on the internal organs with suspicion, and look out for growth or nodules that seem out of place. That carcase is going into the human food chain, be it is for your own consumption or through a game dealer, and responsibility for ensuring that it is fit for the purpose lies with you in the first instance. If in any doubt, bag up your samples carefully and get them to a veterinary examiner.

External Parasites - Ticks, Keds, Lice
It is quite usual to find deer keds on an animal. They look like small, flattened, wingless flies with six legs that scuttle very quickly between the hairs of their host. About 13mm in length, keds initially have wings after pupating on the ground, but these are lost soon after they find a host and start to feed on blood from its skin. Keds are not always immediately apparent when you inspect a freshly-shot animal, but soon start to die and fall off once the carcase cools. Very often the first sign of them is when the dog brings one into the house, or when they transfer to you in search of a new host!

Though unattractive to look at, keds carry no significant diseases and cause no damage to the deer beyond mild irritation. They are easily killed by modern insecticides.

Lice are only about 2mm in length and come in two main types - those that suck blood and those that feed on skin debris. They are wingless and may be seen as a reddish undercoat on the deer, particularly in the groin area. Very often the hair in the infected area is rubbed away. The shedding of the deer's winter coat in spring generally removes much of any louse burden.

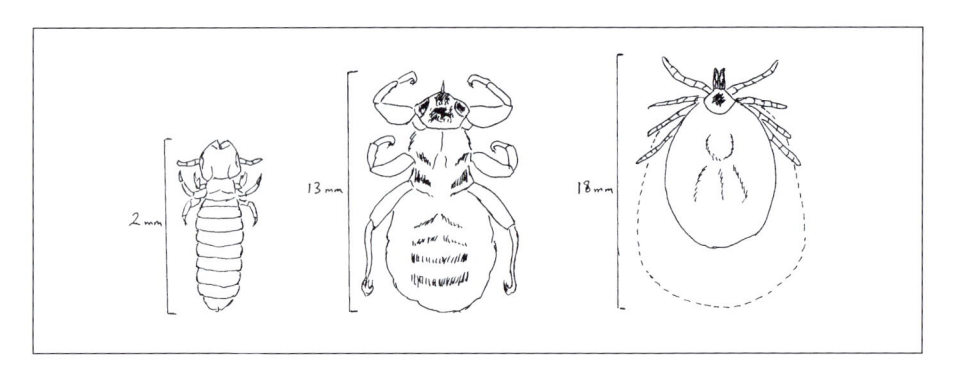

The main external parasites of deer (left to right); louse, ked and castor bean tick (the broken line shows the tick fully fed)

Deer ked

Castor bean ticks feeding in the groin area

Although lice have no real significance in the transmission of diseases, you should not expect to find them on every animal that you shoot. They are relatively rarely found on muntjac, and a heavy louse burden may well be a sign of poor condition.

Ticks are the most significant of the external parasites affecting deer. There are three main species, the most common of which is the castor bean or sheep tick. It is quite usual to find them at various levels of engorgement, normally on the neck, belly, under the legs or behind the ears of an animal, with their heads buried in the skin where they feed on blood. They are particularly abundant in areas where sheep are farmed and where there is dense, warm ground cover such as bracken.

The tick life cycle involves three hosts. The female tick feeds off Host 1 for about two weeks, then drops off and onto the ground where she lays her eggs. As much as a year later, the six-legged tick larva will emerge to feed off Host 2, normally a small rodent or bird, before falling off to moult. After remaining in the ground over winter, the nymph stage (now with a full adult complement of eight legs) eventually emerges and moults again to feed on Host 3 for about a week. It may then fall off to spend as much as a year on the ground before becoming adult.

As ticks are blood suckers and habitually move from host to host, they are capable of transmitting infectious diseases although not all infected animals will show clinical symptoms and most ticks are disease-free. The most important tick-borne illness is Lyme Disease, and the tick is indeed the main vector for the bacterium that causes it. The first sign is a red patch of inflammation around the site of the bite, which spreads over several days. Other signs of human infection could include headache, general malaise and 'flu-type symptoms; eventually arthritis, meningitis or paralysis may occur. Although there have been fatal cases among humans, early treatment with antibiotics is fully effective. If you are bitten by a tick it makes sense to keep an eye on the bite and pay an immediate visit to the doctor if you have any concerns.

Internal Parasites

When the muntjac was transferred to Britain from its Asiatic habitat, it came without its normal internal parasites – mainly because the secondary hosts were left behind. Although susceptible to those found in this country, infestation is extremely rare and very few cases have ever been recorded. Of all the British deer, muntjac are especially resistant to internal parasites, but it always pays to be aware of the signs of the main ones in case anything unusual turns up.

Liver fluke may appear as a mottled surface on the liver. When the liver is cut open, thickened tubes looking like clay pipe stems and chalky deposits will be apparent, and the flukes themselves (looking like rolled-up leaves) can sometimes be seen in the bile ducts. The life cycle of the liver fluke is complex, and dependent on a specific species of snail (which favours marshy ground) to act as the secondary host.

Overcrowding is likely to be the main cause of severe liver fluke infestation and under normal conditions the parasite is of little importance. Any liver found to be affected should be discarded, although the rest of the carcase will be fit for human consumption.

Lung worms resemble short pieces of cotton thread and are about three to five centimetres long. The exterior of an affected lung can have whitish patches or dead-looking grey areas. Unless present in very large quantities, when they can actually block the airway, damage to the lung tissue from worm infestation can make it susceptible to invasion by pathogens which are more likely to cause the death of the deer.

Liver fluke may cause a mottled surface to the liver, and is easily spotted if the liver is cut open. The small leaf-like objects to the right are the flukes themselves.

Lung worms resemble short pieces of cotton thread. Here, one can be seen just below the knife blade.

A tapeworm cyst in the abdominal cavity of a roe deer

An affected animal may cough as a result of the irritation in its lungs, or in an attempt to eject the worms in its airway; it may have a generally debilitated appearance and a scruffy coat. Muntjac are considered to be particularly resistant to lungworm infection, but if in any doubt it is wise to discard the lungs if you are normally in the habit of feeding them to your dog.

If you find a cyst, filled with clear liquid and about the size of a nut, loosely attached within the body cavity of a deer (perhaps on the liver, gut or the wall of the abdominal cavity), chances are that it is the larval stage of a canine tapeworm. Often such cysts can reach the size of a ping-pong ball. Before the life cycle of the tapeworm can progress to the adult stage, the cyst must first be eaten by a carnivore such as a dog or a fox (tapeworm eggs are later passed in their faeces and picked up on vegetation by the feeding deer). Great care therefore needs to be taken when disposing of the gralloch, and dogs should not be fed any infected material. Only heavily infested deer carcases are considered unsuitable for human consumption.

Diseases

As a rule, wild deer are usually healthy. The smaller species tend not to congregate together and so reduce their susceptibility to infection even further, unlike the larger herding deer and particularly domestic stock. I am aware of only one reported case of bovine tuberculosis in a British muntjac, and it is widely felt that badgers remain the most significant self-sustaining wildlife reservoir for it. Deer certainly can provide a vector, and their involvement in the spread of TB is held under constant review. To date, there has been no evidence of brucellosis or rabies in any wild deer in this country. Rinderpest has not been seen for many years, and whilst outbreaks of anthrax killed many deer in mainland Europe during two outbreaks in the 1960s and 1970s, it remains very rare.

Research that followed the 1967-68 outbreak of foot and mouth disease (FMD) proved that all of the British deer were susceptible to the disease, at least under experimental conditions. Reactions were especially severe in the roe and muntjac that were deliberately infected, and six of the nine muntjac in the trial actually died. However, it is noteworthy that none of them showed any signs of the lameness or increased salivation associated with FMD infection that would make it easy to recognise it in an animal 'on the hoof'. It was also found that, although the levels of the virus secreted were high enough to be a potential cause of infection in cattle, only in the droppings of some of the larger deer species did the virus persist long enough for them to be considered as carriers. There were no reported cases of FMD in deer during the 2001 outbreak.

FMD: vesicules on the tongue of a deer (in this case a fallow)

Lesion between the cleaves of the hoof of a muntjac resulting from FMD infection

All of the above are classified as Notifiable Diseases. By law, if you have any suspicion of their presence you must notify the local DEFRA District Veterinary Manager who will arrange for all necessary testing and is an invaluable source of advice. You can find him in the telephone directory or through your local vet.

There are often no external signs that something is wrong, beyond a general wasting of the body or unusual behaviour. You should always be in the habit of checking a shot animal externally and internally for anything unusual. FMD infection, for instance, often appears as sores between the cleaves of the feet or as lesions in the animal's mouth. The best indicator of the need for a closer look is an examination of the lymphatic system, more of which is covered below.

The Lymph Nodes
The lymphatic system is an enormously important indicator of the general health of a deer. Tissue fluid bathes all of the cells in the body, and makes its way into the blood stream by one of two routes. One is through the small capillary blood vessels; the other is via the lymph vessel network. Before this fluid enters the blood vessels it has to pass through lymphatic tissues, some of which are formed into small capsules known as nodes. These nodes act as filters for dust, bacteria and any other foreign bodies and stop them entering the blood stream and any excessive swelling of the node is an indicator that something might be amiss.

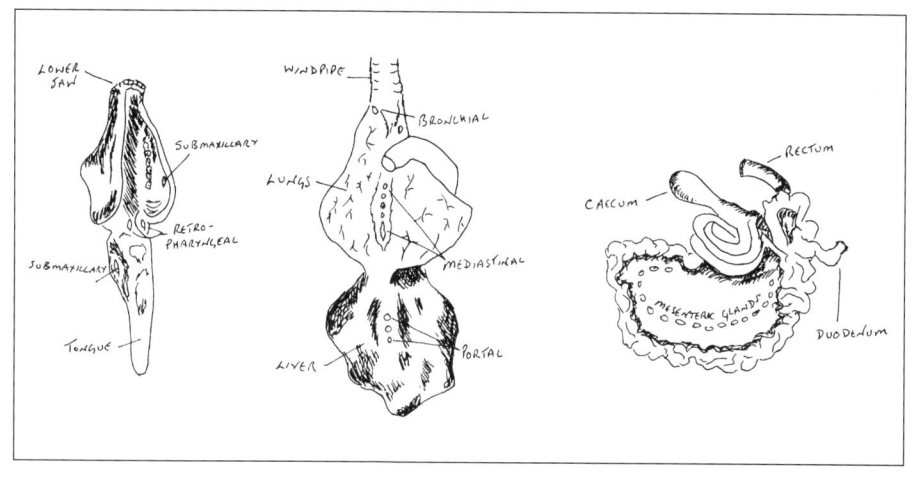

Positions of the lymph nodes in (left to right) the head, the lungs and liver, and the intestine)

The positions of the submaxillary, retro-pharyngeal, bronchial, mediastinal, portal and mesenteric lymph nodes are shown in the accompanying illustrations. It is accepted best practice that all should be inspected by the stalker before the carcase passes into the human food chain. In fact the 'pluck' (i.e. the lungs, liver, spleen and heart) must go to the game dealer with the carcase for veterinary inspection before the latter can be exported.

Some of the nodes can be very difficult to find, especially in an animal as small as a muntjac, and it helps to have them pointed out to you by an experienced stalker. The easiest to find for the novice are the mesenteric, which lie in a line within the intestines as shown in the accompanying photograph. Even if you have no intention of passing the carcase any further than your own kitchen, you should get into the habit of checking them as a bare minimum.

The line of the mesenteric lymph nodes

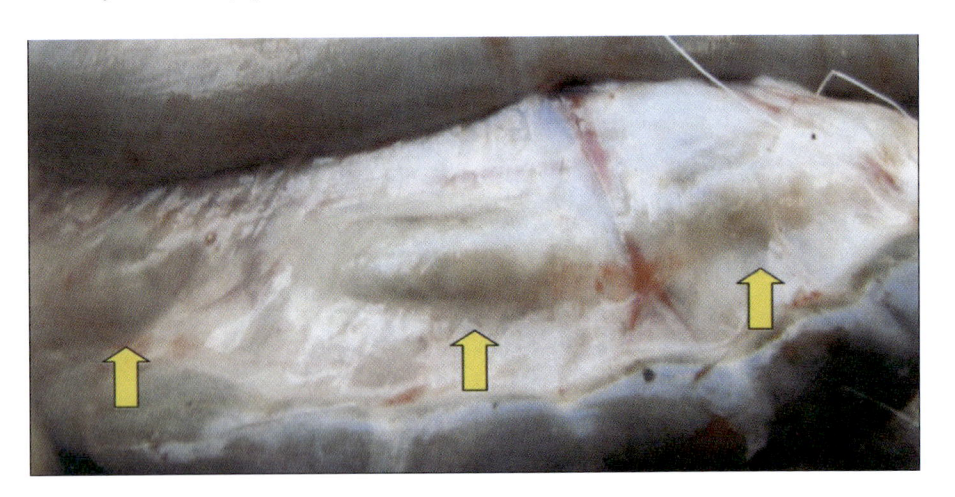

Healthy mesenteric lymph nodes (arrowed). These are the easiest of the lymph nodes to find in an animal as small as a muntjac; swelling, inflammation or discolouration are signs that all may not be as it should.

All of the lymph nodes should be smooth, firm and ovoid or bean-shaped. Any that are obviously swollen, discoloured or grossly misshapen are a potential cause for concern and demand further examination. Don't be tempted to cut them open to see what the inside looks like; if there is any infection there this will only give it the chance to spread it further. What you need to do next is covered in the next section.

Suspect Health – Next Steps
Assuming you have found something that looks suspicious in a carcase, what

steps should you take next? Hopefully you know an experienced stalker who you can consult for a second opinion, but perhaps you may not. In such a case your local vet is a good source of informed knowledge but you will probably have to take the samples to him. Storing his telephone number on your mobile 'phone will allow you to call ahead, and maybe even describe what you have found and have your mind put at rest. He will doubtless advise you on what to do should he be sufficiently worried by what you tell him. If a vet is not available, don't be afraid of approaching the local DEFRA office directly.

When handling suspect organs, it is of the utmost importance that you wear gloves. The simplest approach is to put everything into clean plastic bags (a black bin bag kept in a pocket or your rucksack is ideal for any number of purposes). Smaller samples can be placed in freezer bags or the like, which you will hopefully be carrying anyway for keeping the liver and kidneys in as part of your normal gralloching routine. If you are planning to remove the stomach and intestines a small puncture in the stomach wall will prevent it from ballooning up as bacterial action cause a build-up of gases.

Be careful to ensure that the site is clear before you leave it - suspect grallochs are best destroyed by incineration, but if you have to bury them do it well to prevent other wild creatures from finding and consuming it. Transport the carcase in a clean container separate from any others that you may have shot. Take care that everything is kept cool, but do not freeze samples - this renders them unsuitable for examination and may kill off any micro organisms that might otherwise show up. If you have to temporarily store things at home, make sure that they are not accessible to children or domestic pets.

Speed is of the essence when getting samples to a laboratory. If you are enlisting the assistance of your vet, he will have better facilities to prepare and package them. Otherwise, it is best to keep it simple. Glass or plastic pots and jars can be sterilised with boiling water, and clean plastic bags are an option for larger organs. Don't forget to label everything simply but clearly with the date, location, and any other details that might be pertinent.

Be prepared for a swift response from DEFRA if your suspicions are confirmed by laboratory testing. A recent case of TB found in a roebuck resulted in a thorough decontamination of the site where it was shot, the vehicle in which it was transported and the stalker himself! And remember, if you can't manage to find the place where you shot the animal you are likely to look rather foolish.

You should not go away with the impression that such occurrences are everyday events for stalkers. They are not - most of us will spend a lifetime without having to submit suspect samples for examination. However, as I hope I made clear at the beginning of this chapter, it is the duty of every stalker to know what to do if he discovers anything out of the ordinary.

Oddities

To round off, it might be timely to mention a few oddities that you may come across from time to time. Muntjac frequently injure themselves (and each other) fighting, in road traffic accidents or by other means, and it is astonishing at times that some animals can lead normal lives after recovering from quite serious injuries. Some animals can even lose a limb and still move about normally, running at much their normal speed on only three legs. Occasionally genuine 'freaks' appear, such as an animal with two fully developed hooves at the end of one leg (the condition is known as 'polydactylism').

Scars are commonplace on mature bucks that have received them during fights over territory, as are ripped ears from the same causes. The sharp canine teeth are capable of doing far greater damage to an opponent than the rudimentary, incurved antlers which are employed more in shoving matches when a trial of strength occurs. The slashing canines of a muntjac buck are used quickly and accurately, and are not to be trifled with. A mature buck that is not carrying any obvious injuries from such altercations is usually a more dominant specimen. Broken canines are commonplace by middle age, much to the disadvantage of the owner. Broken antlers, just as common, are at least regrown after casting.

It is quite usual to find bucks with ripped ears, inflicted by the canine tusks of an opponent during fighting.

Antler malformations are not so commonplace, but they do occur. Any buck with more than a single spike, and perhaps a brow tine, is unusual. Damage to the growing antler when still in velvet can bring about some very unusual effects, and damage to the pedicle can cause the antler to grow out of it at a bizarre angle. I am not aware of any instances of hummelism in muntjac. This is a condition more commonly found in red deer, but also very rarely in roe, where the adult buck fails to produce antlers at all. As hummelism is usually linked to failure of the growing animal to reach a threshold body weight before it can develop the pedicles from which the antlers will eventually grow, I believe that it is unlikely to affect an animal as small as the muntjac. However, it is foolish to make hard-and-fast statements about deer, and no doubt there is one waiting out there to prove me wrong.

One of these mature bucks never developed canine tusks, the other only one. Interestingly, the lower buck was shot some five yards from where the other was taken a year later.

An unusual twist in the antler. The cause in this case is uncertain, but may be associated with a calcium deficiency.

This malformation was almost undoubtedly caused by damage to the growing antler whilst still in velvet.

There is no doubt here as to the cause of this malformed antler. The remains of a lead projectile can clearly be seen embedded in the pedicle.

Another example of malformation caused by damage to the growing antler.

Here, secondary antler growth has occurred at the side of the pedicle. Damage to the pedicle itself, from some form of collision or perhaps a shotgun pellet, is the most likely cause.

Campylognathie, or bent-nosed syndrome, has been noted in muntjac. It is a rare phenomenon that results in the nose bones growing at a twisted angle. There is as yet no scientific explanation for the condition, but it may be genetic. Some have suggested that the malformation follows the laws of coriosis, which also dictate which direction that water swirls when it goes down a plug hole. In the northern hemisphere the bend is supposed to be towards the right, and in the southern towards the left. A nice theory, certainly, but the buck in the photograph, shot in the Northampton area, doesn't bear it out!

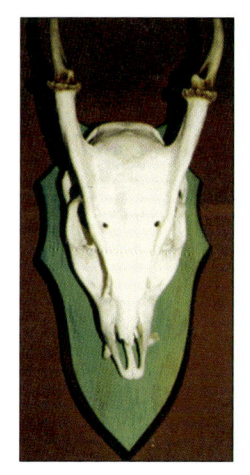

A rare example of campylognathie in a British muntjac

CHAPTER 9
The Future

Muntjac & Man

By 1950, after having half a century to establish themselves in this country, muntjac were still being regarded as an amusing curiosity that presented no real problems of note. Much was made of their Asiatic origins and an associated perception that they were not really resistant to colder British conditions. The seemingly catastrophic die-off during the exceptionally hard winter of 1963 reinforced this view and convinced many that the muntjac had no real future on our island.

Certainly, by the 1960s, their nuisance value to gardeners was beginning to be recognised, but even informed observers remained convinced that little significant damage was being done. By the 1980s, however, perceptions were starting to change and concerns were being raised over browsing and fraying damage to forestry interests. As muntjac numbers have continued to climb, the threat to the environment of having too many muntjac has finally been recognised.

After a fairly bright beginning, muntjac and man are now experiencing a slightly uneasy coexistence. Although still largely welcome within suburban gardens, forestry interests are less sanguine as the potential for large-scale damage is becoming apparent. Farmers and market gardeners, too, are suffering losses where the deer are discovering readily available alternatives to their natural sources of forage. Fortunately domestic livestock is not readily at risk; studies have proven that even where muntjac are susceptible to some of the major diseases, this is in itself uncommon and even then they are extremely unlikely to act as vectors.

The situation is not helped by the fact that the muntjac is positively encouraged by man in many places. Quite apart from the question of illegal introductions, man has created artificial environments where the muntjac thrives. They can exist where other deer species can't or won't. Semi-urban waste ground, embankments and overgrown gardens are all attractive and readily used. Even where a rural landscape is managed for game shooting or other interests, fox control reduces the potential for fawn predation and encourages numbers to build up. It was significant during the 2002 outbreak of Foot and Mouth Disease that, where movement restrictions prevented land access for vermin control, muntjac numbers fell noticeably in some places where fox numbers were permitted to rise. A high density of foxes means a lower density of muntjac.

Road Traffic Accidents are becoming more widespread; indeed, drive any major road in the rural Midlands or eastern counties and you will quickly become aware of the previous night's casualties (and these are only the ones that have been killed outright). Drive the same roads during the hours of darkness and the reason is apparent, with deer feeding in large numbers, apparently unconcerned by the traffic, on the road verges. Very often the first sign of muntjac in an area where no previous records exist is a corpse at the side of the carriageway. To date, no figures have been collated regarding collisions and associated insurance claims involving muntjac, but there is no doubt that they are rising.

So is the muntjac a resource or a liability? It depends on your viewpoint. It has found and filled an ecological niche in Britain, and most problems are stemming from the fact that it has become too successful and outgrown that niche. From tolerant beginnings, we are developing a love-hate relationship with the muntjac. On one hand it is a charming addition to our countryside; at the other extreme it is becoming a pest that some might seek to eradicate.

The truth is that the future of the muntjac lies entirely in our hands and rests on the steps that we take now to confirm its status in Britain and contain its spread. Now, more than ever in the past hundred years, management is the key

There is little interaction between muntjac and domestic livestock, nor are muntjac currently considered to be potentially significant vectors for diseases.

Despite intolerance in some quarters, muntjac still have many admirers.

issue. If we get it right the muntjac will be an undoubted resource. Get it wrong, and the muntjac will become a liability not just to us, but to the other wildlife of our island and ultimately to itself.

Containment or Further Spread?

It is generally accepted that a newly introduced alien species will go through three main phases as it establishes itself in a new environment. The first is basic Establishment, as the species determines whether that environment will support it, and begins to feel secure enough to breed. Having gained a foothold it will go into a Growth phase, as it builds on numbers and the tenuous new population starts to spread. At this point it may discover boundaries which keep it in check and prevent any further build up of numbers - these might include an unsuitable climate, insufficient habitat, efficient predators or direct human intervention. On the other hand, if insufficient natural or artificial boundaries exist, the population moves into the last phase - the Boom, when numbers start to rise rapidly.

Of the many resident species alien to Britain, the rabbit is a clear example of one that reached the last phase without much help. The pheasant does well, although with a good deal of human assistance without which it would struggle to maintain numbers in the face of heavy predation. The wallaby population in the Peak District has never really moved far beyond Establishment as numbers are held in check by the climate. Timely and determined human intervention stopped the muskrat and coypu in their tracks. Of the deer, sika, preferring a specific habitat, found physical boundaries that contained populations even though numbers continue to grow within them. Chinese Water deer, being equally habitat-specific but less robust in the face of our climate, have gone only slightly beyond the Establishment phase so far.

The muntjac, however, has found Britain very much to its liking and is doing very much what the rabbit did when introduced almost a millennium ago. After a long period of establishment and slow growth, the British population (estimated at only some 5,000 in the 1970s) quickly started to boom and now numbers anything between a very conservative 40,000 and 100,000, depending on whose figures you are reading. I strongly suspect that the larger figure is closer to the truth. Britain offers an attractive habitat, it can cope with the climate, predators are few and man has failed to intervene in its spread.

Although foxes are significant predators of muntjac fawns, they offer no real threat to a healthy mature animal

There is no doubt that the muntjac has fully adapted to the British climate

Allowed the opportunity, muntjac will continue to colonise any parts of the country that will support them

The muntjac population will continue to push at the physical boundaries as it grows, adapting along the way. Satellite populations, currently outside the core distribution areas, will eventually join up with the main body. Plenty of suitable habitat exists outside the muntjac's current distribution, just waiting to be filled. By being prepared to tolerate the close proximity of man, the muntjac keeps its options even further open.

Despite legislation restricting the deliberate introduction or translocation of muntjac, these practices continue. Some wish to establish deer for sporting purposes where currently there are none, others may have more sinister motives such as illegal coursing. In addition, well-meaning people are still rehabilitating animals involved in road traffic accidents and returning them to the wild. Whatever the motivations behind it, such human assistance has been a major factor in the rapidly expanding muntjac distribution and must be stopped.

We are now at the stage when only human intervention can control numbers and further spread. There are few natural limitations, and the muntjac has already demonstrated its adaptability although it remains to be seen whether it can cope with the wilder, less hospitable parts of the country, particularly in the west and far north. I believe that it is a fair assessment of the situation to suggest that many parts of the Lowlands of Scotland will be fully colonised within the next decade, along with most of Wales.

The means at our disposal to control muntjac numbers are fairly limited, and shooting is currently the most practical by far. At a local level, it is possible to exclude them from enclosures, gardens or forestry (if only for a while) but this is expensive, has to be done comprehensively if it is to work, and at the end of the day does not physically reduce numbers. Immuno-contraception is still in the experimental stages, though how this would be applied to a free-living wild deer population is a mystery to me. Two major concerns that stem from such an approach are the unquantified effects on other wildlife through the release of chemicals into the environment, and the potential impact on the venison trade.

If we are to get to grips with a burgeoning muntjac population before it slips beyond our control, a more co-operative approach is going to be needed. It is of no use managing the deer on one area diligently, whilst a neighbouring one allows the muntjac to breed unchecked and provide a reservoir for future emigration. This very basic principle applies at local levels up to the national approach. There is no need for a national plan beyond simple encouragement to get on with the job, as there is more than sufficient guidance, training and 'best practice' available already. I have heard the suggestion that a bounty might be paid for muntjac tails, much along the lines of the ill-fated attempt to eradicate the grey squirrel in the 1950s and 1960s. Sadly, a side effect of this initiative was to create a vested interest in maintaining squirrel numbers to ensure that the bounty became a regular source of income!

The way forward has to be the creation of an atmosphere in which the stalker, be he professional or amateur, is actively encouraged to get on with the job of muntjac control. A positive and enlightened approach to firearms legislation is essential. Although I believe that there is nothing wrong with the law as it stands, the interpretation and implementation of it begs improvement at times. Making it possible for more people to become involved in stalking is a start, along with easily accessible stalker training and a developed venison market to pass on the fruits of their labours. More will be said on these latter subjects further on.

Impact on Other Wildlife

As we have seen, the muntjac found itself an empty niche in the British countryside and, until it started to overflow that niche, problems were few. Now it is beginning to impact on other species.

Of the other five deer species, the larger ones are largely unaffected by the presence of muntjac. They are all predominantly bulk feeders, or grazers, and do not have any special requirement for high quality forage. Where they do, their size allows them to browse well beyond the reach of smaller deer. Fallow and muntjac seem the happiest bedfellows, and seem able to share the same areas of woodland without any discernible impact on, or interaction with, the other. The same can be said of relationships with red and sika deer, although the muntjac does not occur so commonly within the current ranges of these former two.

It is the roe that seems most affected by the presence of muntjac. Both are concentrate selectors in their feeding habits - their smaller digestive systems demand high quality fodder which is taken very selectively. Coarser foodstuffs are ignored except in the hardest of times. They browse at much the same heights, and require similar habitats to feel secure and sheltered. Reports of interactions between the two species are varied, but despite its smaller size the muntjac does not seem to be the dominated species. It is true that muntjac and

Where muntjac and roe occur together, relationships between the species tend to be uneasy

roe will frequently pay no attention to each other, but my own observations have shown all sexes and age groups of roe to be noticeably skittish in the presence of muntjac. I have watched large bucks actively drive roe off prime feeding areas, and suggest that in general the muntjac tends to demonstrate greater aggression during the majority of encounters. If comparisons of average body weights show a tendency towards decline over the years, it invariably seems to be the roe that are suffering. In areas that support both roe and muntjac, accurate records are vital and point out important trends to the deer manager. The start of any decline will usually coincide with the point where muntjac have established themselves firmly in a new area, perhaps after a few years presence in lower numbers, and started to multiply significantly.

Browsing damage to bluebells

A clear demonstration of the effect of excessive muntjac numbers. This deer exclosure in a Cambridgeshire nature reserve has allowed a rapid and dramatic regeneration of the woodland floor. Outside it, browsing pressure from muntjac (the only resident deer species) has stifled new growth.

Other wildlife are also affected where muntjac have been allowed to increase out of proportion to their habitat. The woodland understorey can be reduced to the point where ground nesting birds and small mammals are denied cover, invertebrate life on which they depend is reduced, and the eventual dying back of root systems ultimately contributes to the erosion of the ground itself. Although the worst of these effects are by no means imminent, they form a possible scenario that we cannot ignore. In the meantime, it would be foolish in the extreme to permit one species to multiply at the expense of our other flora and fauna.

Commercial Potential
Britain is one of very few places in the world where wild muntjac stalking is readily available to the sportsman. This is becoming increasingly recognised outside our shores, and sportsmen from abroad are deliberately coming to us with the specific purpose of stalking muntjac. As direct result, the value of a trophy buck is slowly increasing. The muntjac has become firmly established as an 'exotic' species with special value as an oddity. A muntjac trophy may not have the 'in your face' magnificence of a red deer stag, or the graceful symmetry of a roe, but it possesses a certain beauty for those who care to see it. There are already those who do, and their numbers are growing.

The special challenge of stalking the muntjac is also becoming recognised. As we have seen, it demands a particular stalking approach and can be the most difficult of our deer to get to grips with on a regular basis. In areas where

A fine buck; increasing numbers of sportsmen are beginning to recognise the special attraction of muntjac stalking

muntjac populations are firmly managed, or have yet to fully develop in size, the experienced stalker need look no further for a challenging quarry. Alternately, in areas with a high density, the beginner can have excellent opportunities to get himself started without much of the expense associated with other forms of stalking.

There are those who look down on trophy or sport hunters, questioning the ethics of hunting an animal purely for its antlers, but I would ask you to consider the contribution that the paying sportsman makes to deer management in general. True, he may not be interested in contributing to the overall cull by shooting does (the true key to controlling numbers) or immature bucks. However, through the money he pays for the right to seek a trophy, he is enabling the landowner to employ a professional whose job it is to complete the real bulk of the cull. Without his fees it would not be possible to maintain a full-time deer manager on many estates.

Although there is always a need to beware exploitation or over-commercialism, the muntjac does not lend himself to being exploited. It is extremely difficult to over-shoot a muntjac population because the deer's own secretive habits will not permit it. However, care must be taken not to neglect the more important aspects of control in favour of those that bring in the paying guests. It is easy to concentrate on the wrong things while neglecting the essential.

While avoiding greed, we live in a commercial world. We must recognise the value of the muntjac as a renewable resource and develop it - not just to our benefit, but also to that of the deer themselves.

The muntjac is increasingly becoming a sporting quarry in its own right

The Venison Market

No matter how widely opinion varies between stalkers – and my goodness how it does at times! – one thing is universally agreed. The venison market in this country is woefully underdeveloped. At the time of writing, the stalker is unlikely to get more than 50p per pound for large deer carcases, and perhaps 75p per pound for roe, and even then these prices tend to fluctuate wildly according to consumer demand or the time of year. Muntjac venison is even more difficult to pass on to the game dealer and some stalkers consider themselves lucky to be offered a price at all. A muntjac carcase is half the size of a roe, and anyone who has skinned one will testify to the extra effort that goes into transforming it into a form ready for the kitchen. The dealers are simply not prepared to make so much effort for so little return.

It shocked me to learn recently that over 80% of the venison shot in this country is exported, mainly to the Continent. What is so wrong with it that the British shopper is not interested? A look at the butchers slab or the supermarket shelf will give you a clue. What started out as being worth a few pence per pound 'in the skin' suddenly becomes a joint costing as much as 1,000% more in a shrink-wrapped tray. At my local farmer's market recently I saw a poorly presented muntjac saddle joint weighing about 1½ lbs (and much of this bone, mind) on sale for £8. Go to the supermarket, and the prices are just as extortionate – if you can find venison there in the first place. The odds are that, if you do, it will be kept with the luxury items or the 'reduced to clear' section because it is approaching its sell-by date and nobody wants it.

The situation is ridiculous. If there is so much venison available that it is worth so little, why is it so overpriced by the time it is offered to the consumer who inevitably sees it as a luxury food that only toffs eat? Perhaps they have tried it once and been put off by a rank joint from a stag that was shot when

Carcases in cold storage awaiting processing

Prepared venison, attractively packaged and ready for the shop shelf or farmer's market

completely spent during the rut, or a shrivelled, overcooked cut prepared by someone who knew no better.

Muntjac venison has everything going for it. Like that of all deer, it is delicious, lean and healthy meat. It lacks the gaminess of some other species; a haunch is a generous supper for four hungry people, a saddle can only be described as sublime, and muntjac mince is so versatile that it will better any recipe which calls for beef mince. Try a muntjac burger and see what I mean! To my mind, and I am certainly not alone in this view, muntjac venison is about the best that you can get. As far as the recreational stalker is concerned, the muntjac is near perfect - it takes up little room in the family freezer, home butchery is not a complicated matter, the taste is acceptable to the children, and a haunch is not so large that it is destined to provide a week of leftovers!

Above all, wild venison of any kind wins hands down when it comes to ethics. Logically, it is easy to see which is the more defensible – livestock farmed and slaughtered under factory conditions, or a wild deer that does not know that it is dead until it falls to a precisely-aimed bullet. Even in today's Disneyfied age, where 'meat' is something that comes in plastic wrapping (and was never covered in fur in the first place) the message needs to get through. Pictures of Bambis on the label do not help, no matter what the marketers think.

There is no question about it, the venison market needs proactive, intelligent development and it is simply waiting for the right approach. Although some forward-thinking game dealers and butchers are trying to do just this, their efforts remain at a local level and national co-ordination is desperately needed if significant results are to be achieved. Venison has to become an everyday meat that the consumer looks at in the same way as lamb, beef, pork or chicken. It must be competitively priced against the day-to-day alternatives, and it needs to be readily available to the shopper in the same way. Reduced price, higher availability, and everyday appeal can only result in one thing - increased demand.

And of course increased demand brings us back to the stalker and the game dealer, who find that they are receiving a price which justifies their efforts. Result? More muntjac shot, numbers reduced, greater control, population in check. It can only be a good thing.

Compulsory Deer Manager Training?
Many countries already insist on a degree of formal training before the novice stalker is allowed out for real. While some of them hold what amount to mini-degree courses, the standards set in others can be laughable to the point of being useless. I will never forget sitting through a morning of theoretical instruction (in a foreign language that I was not fluent in) in one country, to be handed a paper in English for the written exam at the end. It started with

the question 'What is the best way to demonstrate your marksmanship to your fellow hunters? a. On a rifle range, b. On a live target, or c. By shooting the cones off telegraph poles'. The rest of the test was in the same vein, and won me the right to buy a rifle and hunt freely on state land. I won't name the country as this was a few years ago and perhaps things have changed (although I doubt it). But it illustrates the need for standards to be worth enforcing in the first place.

Britain has not gone down the compulsory route yet, and I do not believe that it should. Encouragement should be sufficient – we have enough legislation to cope with as it is, and a desire to do the job well is far more effective than any legal obligation. Deer populations of all species have grown considerably over the last forty years or so, and even the politicians are being forced to take notice by increasing levels of environmental damage, road traffic accidents and the like. It is easy to point out that our attitudes and approach to controlling deer have improved dramatically in recent years. However, a great deal of work needs doing and Britain needs more stalkers who are willing and capable of getting out and doing the job properly. There is no doubt that these newcomers need to be trained – the question is how?

If muntjac numbers are to be kept in check, to the benefit of the environment and the deer themselves, newcomers must be encouraged into taking up stalking.

Whilst I have said that stalker training is not mandatory in this country, in reality this is not entirely true. Some regional police forces are insisting on proof of formal qualifications before they will issue Firearms Certificates (although there is no requirement for this under the law), and many landowners (rightfully mindful of their obligations under Health & Safety legislation) are doing the same before they will allow a stalker onto their land. So while we do not yet have compulsory training yet, the obligation exists. I leave it for you to decide whether the forces that drive it are just or not. The bottom line is that the newcomer is already strongly encouraged to obtain a certificate of some kind to prove their competence.

Not everyone has access to an experienced mentor to take him through a stalking apprenticeship. The key has got to be making stalker training more accessible. The British Deer Society introduced the Woodland Stalkers Course in the 1980s; this evolved into the National Stalkers Competence Certificate which was itself superseded by the present Deer Stalking Certificate Level 1. Now a national standard, this provides excellent entry-level training for the novice and puts him on the right path towards best practice. Formal training costs time and money, of course, and not everyone is able to put aside a block of four of five days to attend a residential course. The BDS is once again taking the initiative, and the bulk of DSC1 is now available as a distance-learning package with the student only required to turn up for final testing.

This is an excellent way forward, but can we do more? Providing training is expensive – people must rightly be reimbursed for making their time, effort and hard-won knowledge available. Most do it gladly for a pittance, but there are some who are making unnecessarily large amounts of money out of it and giving stalker training a bad name. Reducing the cost to the student will increase willingness to undertake, and thus the demand for, training. Perhaps, after all, the politicians can help here – if deer numbers are becoming a national problem, why should the training to enable more people to control deer not be subsidised?

National standards of voluntary training are a first-class start. For many students this is all the training that they will ever do and they will remain sport stalkers for the rest of their involvement with deer. This is fine; we need them. They will help to keep deer numbers in check, and in doing so will help provide the funds that allow professional managers to be employed. Others will catch the 'deer bug' and actively seek out more and more knowledge. They are the intelligent deer managers of the future, and we need them too. Encouragement to learn, and access to realistically priced high-quality training, are the keys to meeting our needs.

A Need for Legislation?
Broadly speaking, the existing law as it relates to wild deer serves the purpose well. It lays a foundation for humane management with suitable weapons, and all that remains is the need to enforce it rigorously and intelligently. As we have seen, the muntjac's aseasonal breeding cycle makes it impossible to legislate for a closed season to avoid orphaning dependant young, so the onus must be on the stalker to ensure that his culling activities are ethically defensible. In the

meantime, it is proper standards and methods that need encouragement, and everyone - from government bodies to national societies and individual stalkers - have their own parts to play.

In any case I am wary of over-legislation. Too much restrictive red tape stifles effort and puts people off doing a job in the first place, especially if that job is a voluntary effort. It is essential that muntjac control must be carried out, and becoming clear that more of it is necessary if we are to properly control numbers. We need to be realistic; of course we must ensure safety, humane culling and the hygienic entry of wild venison into the human food chain, but I am satisfied that the current demands made of the stalker cater for these aspects.

Despite this, there are changes afoot at the time of writing. European regulations on game meat standards are in the pipeline, although it is impossible to forecast the full extent of what they will eventually demand. There is already talk of a need for one member of a 'hunting team' (a term which itself demands further definition) to attend a formal game handling course. Presumably such a regulation is aimed at formal game shooting events where there will be a gamekeeper to deal with the processing of shot birds. How such a rule will affect the lone stalker has yet to be adequately explored. Inevitably, practices that are acceptable to Europe are a 'must' so long as we are so dependent on the venison export trade, but one wonders what else will follow.

The suitability of some of the .22 centrefire calibres, already legal for roe deer in Scotland, is also under discussion with regard to being made legal for shooting the small deer species in England and Wales. I must confess to being of two minds on this issue. On one side, I have no doubt that that these calibres are suitable for culling a deer the size of a muntjac. The Scottish experience with roe bears this view out. Furthermore, a smaller calibre, coupled with a sound moderator, would be especially useful for dealing with problems areas on the edge of suburbia. In such places special safety considerations and the reduction of noise disturbance are of paramount importance.

Yet I remain unconvinced. Although small bullets travelling very fast break up more easily, they are less likely to produce a wound that leaves a workable blood trail and following up a wounded animal becomes much more difficult. Furthermore, what is to say that they will not be used against a larger species if an opportunity presents itself and the temptation is too great? The mainstream entry-level calibre under current law, the .243 Winchester, serves our purposes very well under most circumstances and my gut feeling is that we should leave the .22 centrefires well alone. There is no real benefit in changing the law, and this act in itself would give our legislators a chance to fiddle even further with what they deem to be suitable. Who knows, we could even end up with proscribed calibres and yet more regulations to make an already demanding task even more difficult.

Stalking with a rifle is without doubt the most humane way to manage muntjac

So much hangs in the balance, and our future practices will ultimately be determined by our abilities to keep muntjac numbers in check now. I have expressed my feelings on the suitability of shotguns for muntjac culling elsewhere. Whilst they are already permitted under very specific circumstances already, I would not wish to see more widespread use. In skilled hands, with a proper shot load and used with self-discipline only at close ranges, of course a shotgun will kill a muntjac outright, but the law cannot specify for humane management without first demanding formal training and proof of ability. Of equal importance is a need for selective shooting – and how many people will be able to recognize that a doe might have a dependant fawn in the split second that a fleeting target in cover gives them?

Already there are suggestions being made that muntjac can be driven to rifles in the Continental manner. Apart from the fact that muntjac are not readily moved from their strongholds, we will lose the desired selectivity that we get from conventional stalking means and 'shooting moving' will inevitably mean more wounded animals. Furthermore, the British countryside with its 'Right to Roam' has too high a human population for safety to be guaranteed. The idea is just not a starter.

Night shooting is another issue for the future. Certainly muntjac are more inclined to leave cover at night rather than in daylight, and are relatively easy to shoot in the light of a high powered lamp. But do we really need, or want, to shoot them like rabbits or foxes? Quite apart from the safety issue of high

Only careful study allows the stalker to decide whether or not a doe is likely to have a dependant fawn hidden nearby. This is not possible in the split-second available when muntjac are driven to shotguns or rifles, and equally difficult at night by the light of a spotlight

velocity rifles being discharged at night (when backstops for a bullet are less apparent), selective culling goes out of the window once again. And muntjac are far more robust that a fox. If not struck properly in a vital organ, they are more than likely to make off - and following up a wounded animal can be well nigh impossible in the dark.

As far as means of control are concerned, the responsibility for the future lies with us, the stalkers and deer managers. Muntjac numbers have to be controlled now, using the means and methods already proven to be suitable as well as ethical. If not, less attractive approaches will be forced on us out of sheer necessity if numbers are allowed to get out of hand.

An Established Species

I am very aware that I have posed a number of questions but not supplied that many hard and fast answers. However, the picture is not as gloomy as it might seem, and the future for the muntjac in Britain can be bright if we care to make it so. Muntjac are still capable of being both an attractive and acceptable part of our native fauna, but only if we trouble to keep numbers in check. It is all a question of balance, and recognising that a problem ignored will not go away - as King Canute discovered, you cannot hold back the tide. We are at the point now where eradication is out of the question, and a continued increase in distribution will only be limited by natural barriers. We can,

Love them or hate them, muntjac are here to stay

however, contain the muntjac at a level that the environment can support and man's activities can tolerate through a thoughtful and effective process of control.

If your part of England, Wales or lowland Scotland does not contain muntjac yet, stand by - the chances are that they are on the way. After an absence of some 15 million years, when it died out in Europe and retreated to its Asian strongholds, the muntjac has finally returned. The chances are that it will still be with us until the next Ice Age, and it is only thanks to man that this is so. I am convinced that recognising them as an asset and controlling them through the use of enlightened and humane stalking practices will mean that they can remain welcome.

Study of the muntjac in any detail cannot fail to engender a deep respect for such an interesting, resilient, adaptable and truly delightful little deer. We still have so much to learn about them. It is now up to us to treat the muntjac with respect as a firmly established British species.

APPENDIX 1

FURTHER READING AND CONTACTS

Books

There is very little literature devoted to the muntjac, at least certainly not in the English language. The following are a start:

MUNTJAC Norma Chapman and Stephen Harris (The Mammal Society and the British Deer Society, 1996). One of a series of excellent booklets covering the natural history of British deer.

MUNTJAC Eileen A Soper (Longmans, 1969). An account of the study of muntjac living in and around the author's Hertfordshire garden. Slightly dated now, but still fascinating reading and delightfully illustrated. Although out of print it is worth searching for.

Muntjac, and some of the issues surrounding them, are covered to various degrees in the following works:

DEER Norma Chapman (Whittet Books, 1991) A comprehensive guide to the origins and habits of the deer of Britain.

DEER WATCH Richard Prior (Swan Hill Press, 1987) Although written 17 years ago and republished in 1993, this remains a very useful guide to British deer.

DEER: LAW AND LIABILITIES Charlie Parkes & John Thornley (Swan Hill Press, 2000) Essential reading for anyone who stalks, or has responsibility for the management of deer in the United Kingdom.

GARDENS & DEER Charles Coles (Swan Hill Press, 1997) A guide to damage limitation, including varieties of protection, deterrents, and particular problem areas.

THE NATURAL HISTORY OF DEER Rory Putman (Helm, 1988). Currently out of print but I believe that a revised version may be in the pipeline. A detailed overview of deer origins, behaviour and natural history – highly recommended.

THE DEER MANAGER'S COMPANION Rory Putnam with Dr Jochen Langbein (Swan Hill Press, 2003). A guide to the management of deer in the wild and in parks, written on a scientific (but readable) basis and bringing together many results of recent research.

DEER MANAGEMENT – QUALITY IN SOUTHERN ENGLAND Dominic Griffith (privately published, 2004). A personal approach by a professional deer manager. Although primarily concerned with roe deer, muntjac receive their own chapter and a sizeable element covers muntjac trophy measurement and standards.

TREES & DEER Richard Prior (Swan Hill Press, 1994) Particular emphasis on the management of deer of all species from a forestry perspective.

THE SPORTING RIFLE Robin Marshall-Ball (Swan Hill Press, 2000 (4th edition)) A comprehensive reference work for the rifleman.

THE WHITEHEAD ENCYCLOPEDIA OF DEER G Kenneth Whitehead (Swan Hill Press, 1993) A huge and essential reference work covering all aspects of deer biology, behaviour, stalking and related subjects across the world. Now sadly out of print in book form, but still readily available on CD-ROM.

DEER OF THE WORLD Valerius Geist (Swan Hill Press, 1999) A detailed and scholarly examination of deer evolution and behaviour.

TRAINING DOGS FOR WOODLAND STALKING Guy Wallace (Fawley Publications, 1994, revised 1998) A specialist booklet from one of Britain's foremost dog trainers.

DISEASE ID CARDS (BDS) A set of laminated cards with clear photographs and descriptions of the main deer diseases and parasites, contained in a neat plastic wallet. An invaluable reference guide or training aid for the field.

ROAD TRAFFIC ACCIDENTS AND THE HUMANE DISPATCH OF DEER (BDS & BASC) An Advice Note giving detailed guidance on all aspects of dealing with this potentially sensitive subject. Strongly recommended to anyone who is likely to be called out to deal with a deer RTA.

For the cook, I can recommend two recipe books in particular:

THE VENISON COOK Diane and Nicholas Dalton (Crowood Press, 1991) 106 recipes, all well presented and ranging from the everyday to fare for special occasions.

VENISON COOKERY (Swan Hill Press, 2003) An American title republished in this country, offering a transatlantic approach with some different and innovative ideas.

Most of the above books, as well as many others, can be obtained through British Deer Society Sales. You can view their catalogue and place orders online at www.bds.org.uk. Otherwise, they can be contacted at Sales Office, BDS, Burgate Manor, Fordingbridge, Hampshire SP6 1EF (Telephone: 01425 655434).
Both new and out of print books can be obtained from Coch-y-Bonddu Books, Pentrerhedyn Street, Machynlleth, Powys SY20 8DJ (Telephone: 0870 3002004). Their website (www.anglebooks.com) has an excellent search facility if you are looking for something special.

For those with a specific interest in woodland protection, the Forestry Commission issues a series of Practice and Information Notes. The following are especially useful to the deer manager:

Practice Note No 3: The Prevention of Mammal Damage to Trees in Woodland
Practice Note No 6: Managing Deer in the Countryside
Practice Note No 9: Recommendations for Fallow, Roe and Muntjac Deer Fencing: New Proposals for Temporary and Reusable Fencing
Information Note No 36: The Impact of Deer on Woodland Biodiversity

Forestry Commission Practice and Information Notes can be obtained free as a download from their website www.forestry.gov.uk or by contacting: Forestry Commission Publications, PO Box 25, Weatherby, West Yorkshire LS23 7EW (Telephone: 0870 1214180).

Videos, DVDs and CD-ROMs

There are a wealth of videos (and, increasingly, DVDs) covering all aspects of deer and stalking. Some useful ones for the muntjac stalker are:

The Muntjac and Chinese Water Deer (KRD Wildlife Productions Ltd) Some high quality footage covering aspects of the daily lives of both species.

Britain's Deer (KRD Wildlife Productions Ltd) A guide to the six wild species of deer resident in Britain.

Carcase Preparation and Examination for DSC2 (KRD Wildlife Productions Ltd) Clear and detailed guidance, pitched at the DSC2 student. Includes a particularly good section on inspection of the lymph glands. It leads directly into.....

Venison Carcase Cutting for the Table (KRD Wildlife Productions Ltd) Full instruction on how to turn a carcase into prepared venison for the kitchen, based on larger species of deer and providing as much detail as the muntjac stalker will ever need.

Gralloching and Lardering for DSC2 (BDS production) A fully up-to-date guide, once again aimed at the DSC2 student, and promoting acknowledged best practice at the time of writing.

For those contemplating attending a DSC1 course, or indeed anyone with an interest in deer, the following CD-ROM is highly recommended:

DEERQUEST (Deer-UK) An interactive, computer-based training aid which covers all of the questions you are likely to be faced with in the DSC1 written test. A wrong answer prompts text, photographs, video footage or sound recordings, or a mixture of all four, to explain the right one. Absorbing as well as very educational.

Videos and CD-ROMs can be obtained from British Deer Society Sales (see under Books as above for the address). KRD Wildlife Productions Ltd products are available direct from The Wesleyan Church, Gussage Saint Michael, Near Wimborne, Dorset BH21 5HY (Telephone: 01258 840637) or their website: www.deerdata.co.uk

The Internet

With the growth of the Internet, information on muntjac is now widely available from sources worldwide. Simply type in 'muntjac' and let your search engine do the rest. Variations on the theme – including Latin names – will yield yet more results. Some recommended sites to start with are:

Deer-UK www.deer-uk.com. A sort of 'Internet magazine' for deer managers, stalkers and indeed anyone with an interest in deer. The site contains articles, correspondence, advice, product reviews and a great deal more. Some very comprehensive pages covering the British deer species.

Animal Info www.animalinfo.org An excellent starting point if you are looking for information on the various muntjac species.

Deer Parks and Zoos

Muntjac can be seen in many zoos and collections across the UK. The following selection all offer good viewing opportunities (listed from north to south):

Scottish Deer Centre, Rankeilour Park, Bow of Fife, by Cupar, Fife KY15 4NQ (Telephone: 01337 810391) Easily visible muntjac, some very tame, in a large, natural enclosure.

Blackpool Zoo, East Park Drive, Blackpool, Lancashire FY3 8PP (Telephone: 01253 830830) A large, enclosed paddock where the deer show themselves readily. As the public can only view them from one side, the muntjac feel secure and are very tolerant of human presence.

Woburn Deer Park, Woburn, Bedfordshire MK17 9WA (Telephone: 01525 292148) Healthy numbers of wild muntjac inhabit the park where they were first introduced into this country, and are best seen in the less open areas during the earlier half of the morning or in late afternoon. Many other species of deer as well, in a magnificent parkland setting.

Whipsnade Wild Animal Park, Dunstable, Bedfordshire LU6 2LF (Telephone: 01582 872171) Free-roaming muntjac can be seen throughout the park, frequently entering some of the enclosures housing more exotic species. It is best to arrive before the majority of the public as the animals become more retiring once the crowds build up; whilst tolerant of people, they can be quite skittish.

The Tamar Otter Sanctuary, North Petherwin, Near Launceston, Cornwall PL15 8LW (Telephone: 01566 785646) Free-roaming muntjac within an 18 acre wood, shared with fallow deer. All are very tolerant of the public whilst not petting-tame.

Equipment Suppliers

Stalking equipment can be obtained from any number of sources throughout the UK. If you are having trouble finding something, try:

British Deer Society Sales (see under Books) For targets, calls, stalking sacks and Roesafes etc.

Jägersport, PO Box 32T, Petersfield, Hampshire GU31 5AF (Telephone: 01730 263477) A comprehensive source of stalking equipment and clothing - everything short of rifles and ammunition.

Courses

The primary deer stalker and deer manager training courses available in the UK are:

Deer Stalking Certificate Level 1 An entry-level course which comprehensively covers all the background knowledge and basic skills that any stalker ought to have before going into the field.

Deer Stalking Certificate Level 2 The follow-up qualification to DSC1, based on practical performance in the field.

BDS Deer Managers Course An intensive course that teaches the principles of managing (rather than just stalking) wild deer in the UK. Of immense value to anyone responsible for a wild deer population.

Further information on these courses, including dates, locations and prices, can be obtained from HQ BDS or BASC (DSC1 & 2 only) or on their relevant websites. See below for contact details.

Trophy Measurement

There are a number of accredited CIC trophy measurers scattered across the country. If you shoot a buck and want to see if it has achieved medal status, you will be able to find out the closest to you by accessing the UK CIC website at: www.cictrophy.com

Alternately, HQ BDS will be able to advise you of a suitable contact.

Societies and Organisations

British Deer Society See the separate appendix for a more detailed description of the Society:

The British Deer Society, Burgate Manor, Fordingbridge, Hampshire SP6 1EF
Telephone: 01425 655434   E-mail: h.q@bds.org.uk
Website: www.bds.org.uk

British Association for Shooting and Conservation For the specific department dealing with deer matters:

British Association for Shooting and Conservation (Deer), Marford Mill, Rossett, Wrexham LL12 0HL
Telephone: 01244 573047   E-mail: alan.mccormick@basc.org.uk
Website: www.basc.org.uk

Deer Initiative A national organisation comprising a broad partnership of statutory, voluntary and private interests dedicated to 'ensuring the delivery of a sustainable, well-managed wild deer population in England and Wales'. The website contains some very useful downloads for the deer manager:

The Deer Initiative, PO Box 2196, Wrexham LL14 6YH
Telephone: 0870 774 3677   E-mail: mailto:alan.mccormick@basc.org.ul info@thedeerinitiative.co.uk
Website: www.thedeerinitiative.co.uk

Countryside Alliance The principal UK organisation campaigning for the countryside, country sports and the rural way of life:

The Countryside Alliance, 367 Kennington Road, London SE11 4PT
Telephone: 020 7840 9200   E-mail: news@countryside-alliance.org
Website: www.countryside-alliance.com

APPENDIX 2

MUNTJAC RECIPES

We use a lot of muntjac venison at home; it does not have the more distinctive taste of, say, roe venison, and lends itself to many recipes where you might have otherwise used beef. Its more delicate flavour also allows the use of lighter seasonings, spices and herbs. True cooks may blanch to hear that we use this delicious meat with cook-in sauces and for curries, but where a quick and easy meal is required muntjac is very versatile.

Muntjac venison also processes well to produce a superb mince. Sometimes a little oil or bacon helps to stop it drying out too fast when cooking - it is very lean in comparison to many other meats. A good dash of milk can help to keep things moist.

Don't forget the offal. The heart produces a rich mince, or can be stuffed. The liver is more delicate than that of lamb and can be used for any number of recipes; the simplest way to cook it is to slice it, coat in flour and fry in butter. We tend to stockpile kidneys in the freezer until we have enough to devil them, but why not try a venison & kidney pie?

The following recipes are among our favourites at home; they are all relatively uncomplicated and produce superb results. You can find more in the 'Further Reading' appendix. Both of the recommended books have been extensively trialled in our kitchen and contain some first-class ideas that will delight all tastes.

Sara's Simple Saddle

This is a very uncomplicated way of cooking a saddle, and the results are sublime. It works equally well on other sorts of venison, but you do need to adjust the cooking times when using larger quantities.

muntjac saddle
olive oil
salt and freshly-ground black pepper – to taste
redcurrant jelly - 1 tablespoon
juniper berries, crushed - 8-12 (optional)
gin - 1 capful (optional)

Preheat the oven to 180°C/325°F/Gas Mark 4

Place the saddle (top side upwards) on a square of kitchen foil. Wipe a little olive oil over the meat to give a light covering (venison has little fat and needs to be kept moist when cooking). Season to taste with salt and pepper.

Distribute the juniper berries and redcurrant jelly across the top of the saddle and drizzle the gin over the top. Although the gin and juniper berries are optional, they compliment each other well, add a bit of extra moisture, and give a delicate juniper flavour to the roast.

Wrap the saddle loosely in the foil, place in a baking tray and roast for 1 hour (this will produce well-done meat - reduce the time if you prefer it slightly pink). Carve and serve immediately. You can use the meat juices to make a delicious gravy (don't be ashamed to cheat; you can add the juice to Bisto or similar).

Roast Haunch of Muntjac

A haunch is a generous meal for four to six people. Although you can marinade the meat overnight beforehand, we don't bother to, as quite frankly the meat does not need it. The haunch is prepared in the same way as the saddle (above), perhaps using a good splash of red wine to replace the gin and juniper berries. Alternately, it can be wrapped in fatty bacon - the important thing is to prevent it from drying out when cooking.

Once again loosely wrapped in kitchen foil to prevent the meat from drying out, simply roast on a baking tray at 180°C/325°F/Gas Mark 4 for an hour to an hour and a half, depending on how well done you like the meat to be. Using the juices as the basis for gravy, serve with roast or mashed potatoes and green vegetables.

Pan-Fried Muntjac Steaks

Although muntjac haunches are too small to produce large steaks in the traditional style, by removing the meat from the bone and cutting slices about an inch thick across the grain you can produce some wonderful medallions of meat (there is no need to separate them before cooking) which make a quick and easy meal. The optional sauce is a simple and delicious (if rather cholesterol-heavy) addition.

muntjac steaks
butter or margarine
freshly-ground black pepper – to taste
double cream $^1/_4$ pint (optional)
Drambuie liqueur - one or two tbsps, to taste (optional)

Melt the butter in a flat-bottomed frying pan and add the steaks. Season to taste with the pepper and fry for about five minutes on either side, depending on how well done you prefer them.

For the optional sauce, simply remove the steaks from the pan but leave the juices and melted butter. Add the cream and Drambuie and bring rapidly to the boil stirring continuously. Add a little cornflour if you prefer the sauce thicker. Pour over the steaks and serve.

The following recipes have all been supplied by Cyndy Brown, who was provided with some basic muntjac mince and an amount of better-quality haunch and neck off-cuts, along with instructions to come up with 'something slightly different'. The results are all highly recommended and work just as well in the kitchen as they do on the barbecue:

Moroccan-style Burgers

venison mince - 300 g
pine nuts - 10g
apricots, chopped, dried, 'ready to eat' – 50 g
onion, small, finely chopped – 1
garlic, chopped – 1 clove
cumin, ground – 1 tsp
salt and freshly-ground black pepper – to taste

Dry-fry the pine nuts in a hot frying-pan until golden brown. Watch, as they will burn very quickly if you are not careful.

Tip the nuts, with all other ingredients, into a large bowl and mix thoroughly.

Take a teaspoonful of the mix and cook quickly in a hot frying-pan. Taste, and adjust seasoning as required.

Once happy with the taste take the remaining mixture and, using floured hands, form it into burgers of the required size. Place on a floured plate and chill for at least 30 minutes. Remove the burgers from the fridge about 20 minutes before cooking to allow them to come up to room temperature.

Cook for 7-10 minutes per side, depending on thickness. They go very well with Onion Rice.

Onion Rice

Cook approx 250g Basmati rice by your preferred method. While the rice is cooking, fry an onion in a little olive oil or butter until golden – don't over-brown. Add 2-3 tsp black onion seeds. Add to the drained rice and stir well.

'Trad with a twist' Burgers

venison mince - 300 g
juniper berries, crushed – 12-15
eating apple, medium, peeled, cored, and chopped – 1
thyme, dried – $^1/_2$ tsp
Worcester Sauce – a generous tsp
black onion seeds – $^1/_2$ tsp

salt and freshly-ground black pepper – to taste
streaky bacon, finely chopped – 2 rashers (this is optional, but does give a delicious extra taste and juiciness to the burgers)

Tip all ingredients into a large bowl and mix thoroughly.

Take a teaspoonful of the mix and cook quickly in a hot frying-pan. Taste, and adjust seasoning as required.

Once happy with the taste take the remaining mixture and, using floured hands, form it into burgers of the required size. Place on a floured plate and chill for at least 30 minutes. Remove the burgers from the fridge about 20 minutes before cooking to allow them to come up to room temperature.

Cook for 7-10 minutes per side, depending on thickness. Serve on sesame seed burger buns with Home-made Tomato Sauce.

Home-made Tomato Sauce

Brown a medium onion in a little olive oil or butter. Add a chopped clove of garlic, a little salt and freshly-ground pepper. Cook for a couple of minutes, and then add 400g plum tomatoes (whole or chopped) and a heaped tsp of sugar. Mix thoroughly, and add 2 tsps Worcester Sauce and 2 tbsps tomato puree. Cook over a medium heat, with the lid on, for about 30 mins and then taste and adjust seasonings. If the sauce is still too liquid cook briskly, with the lid off, for a further 10 minutes or until the required consistency is reached.

Venison Kebabs

Muntjac, or other venison, cut into 2-3cm cubes – 500g
baby onions, halved or quartered – 8 to 10
bay leaves, fresh – 8 to 10
thyme sprigs, fresh – a handful
garlic – 1 clove, chopped
olive oil – 1 tbsp
black pepper, freshly ground
red wine

Put all ingredients, except the onions and the bayleaves, into a bowl and add enough red wine to almost cover. Leave to stand for at least an hour, and for 2 – 3 hours if possible, in the 'fridge, stirring occasionally.

Drain the meat, and then thread it onto skewers (if using wooden skewers, remember to soak them in water for a couple of hours before threading with the meat - this will help prevent them burning on the grill), adding a piece of onion and a bay leaf after every 3 or 4 cubes of meat. Leave to stand for 20 – 30 minutes, to allow to reach room temperature, and then barbecue for about 10 minutes, turning occasionally. Very good with Onion Rice and Home-made Tomato Sauce.

APPENDIX 3

DEER STALKING – A Code of Practice

Produced jointly by the British Association for Shooting & Conservation and the British Deer Society

Endorsed by: The Deer Initiative and the Deer Commission for Scotland

INTRODUCTION

This Code of Practice has been produced to provide an introductory guide to deer stalking. Although much of this code is applicable to stalking in the Highlands it has been written primarily with the Lowland woodland shooter in mind. This is because the Highland 'rifle' generally has the benefit of the help and guidance of a professional stalker, while the woodland stalker is more often on his own.

THE NEED FOR DEER CULLING

Deer stalking is a sport but it is also a necessary task for the protection of agricultural crops and forestry and, indeed, of the deer. Deer are prolific breeders and, if numbers are allowed to increase unchecked, damage can result and the deer themselves may become prey to starvation and disease. The culling of deer should always take place as part of a deer management plan which considers all these influencing factors. Wherever appropriate, the management plan should involve close liaison and co-operation between neighbouring landowners and stalkers.

THE DEER STALKER'S OBLIGATIONS

Always remember that your quarry has a strong emotive appeal to many people with little knowledge of deer management. They will judge deer control by your behaviour.

The weapon you are using is capable of killing over great distances and every shot taken must be totally safe. A responsible stalker will have third party liability insurance, but the best insurance is responsible weapon handling.

It is the stalker's responsibility to know, and understand, the laws relating to the sport and, in particular, to be able to identify deer and to know when and where to shoot. The responsible stalker will, in addition, observe the Country Code at all times.

KNOWLEDGE AND EXPERIENCE

All stalkers should aim to gain knowledge and experience not only in the practice of stalking, but also in the ecology of the deer. This can be gained either through recognised training courses or the expert guidance of an experienced stalker or a combination of both. Stalkers can demonstrate a level of competence through attainment of the Deer Stalking Certificate.

In March 2003 the government reaffirmed its position that attainment of deerstalker competence certificates should be voluntary.

CONSIDERATION FOR DEER

Although deer are comparatively large animals, the vital areas for clean kills are small. No one should consider stalking unless he or she can consistently shoot a group of not less than three shots within a 10cm target at 100m.

A shot should be taken at a range to ensure a humane kill. Shots should never be taken at a moving or badly positioned deer, in poor visibility, through cover, or at any time when your aim is not 'steady'. After taking a shot, always assume that you have hit the deer until you have proved otherwise by thorough searching. Always follow up and humanely despatch a wounded deer, regardless of the time and effort involved.

DEER AND THE LAW

The law regarding the killing and taking of deer is not consistent throughout the UK. In both Scotland and Northern Ireland the legislation is different from that governing England and Wales.

In summary, the following are some of the more important provisions, but this is NOT to be taken as a complete or authoritative statement of the law.

Although the Deer Acts and Orders contain exceptions, particularly to allow occupiers to protect their crops (certain conditions apply) from excessive damage, and to permit mercy killing of an animal to prevent suffering, the stalker may NOT...

Use anything except legal firearms to kill deer

Shoot out of season (see Table of Close Seasons)

Shoot at night (one hour after sunset to one hour before sunrise)

Shoot from a vehicle (a moving vehicle in Scotland) or use a vehicle to drive deer (vehicle includes aircraft)

Sell venison except to a licensed game dealer (in England, Wales and Northern Ireland) or a licensed venison dealer (in Scotland)

A Game Licence is needed to kill or take deer, except on enclosed land by the owner or occupier, or with their permission.

FIREARMS AND AMMUNITION

The responsible stalker must only use a rifle and ammunition which are legal for the species of deer being shot. In addition to compliance with the law the stalker should be guided by knowledge, experience and preference in their choice of a rifle and ammunition. The legal requirements are laid down in the several Deer Acts and Orders previously mentioned. For example:

England, Wales and Northern Ireland
For deer of any species, a minimum calibre of .240 inches (.236 inches in Northern Ireland) and a minimum muzzle energy of 1,700 foot pounds is the legal requirement. In Northern Ireland the minimum bullet weight is 100 grains.

Scotland
For deer of any species, the bullet must weigh at least 100 grains AND have a minimum muzzle velocity of 2,450 feet

per second AND a minimum muzzle energy of 1,750 foot pounds.
or
For roe deer, the bullet must weigh at least 50 grains AND have a minimum muzzle velocity of 2,450 feet per second AND a minimum muzzle energy of 1,000 foot pounds.

It must be stressed that all these figures are the minimum legal requirement.

In all the above areas the bullet must be of a type designed to expand/deform on impact.

To ensure safe and humane shooting the stalker must practise and maintain his or her skill with the rifle and must check at regular intervals that his or her rifle is still zeroed correctly - ie that the bullet is striking a selected point of aim at a chosen range.

The rifle must ALWAYS be test-fired, and the zero verified or corrected after a knock or other impact, or after any unaccountably 'wild' shot. No one should continue stalking in such a case, until this zeroing (or 'sighting-in') has been done.

OTHER EQUIPMENT AND AIDS

A responsible stalker will always carry:
a telescope or binoculars for the correct identification of quarry. They will NOT use the rifle 'scope' for this purpose
a serviceable knife of appropriate design
a torch, if stalking in the evening to look for hair or blood signs
a stick, about the same height as the stalker, to steady the forward hand.

A woodland stalker is well advised to have access to a dog trained to locate dead or wounded deer but 'steady' to other wildlife.

STATUTORY CLOSE SEASON FOR DEER (all dates inclusive)

Species	Sex	Eng & Wales	Scotland
Red	M	1 May - 31 July	21 Oct - 30 June
	F	1 Mar - 31 Oct	16 Feb - 20 Oct
Fallow	M	1 May - 31 July	1 May - 31 July
	F	1 Mar - 31 Oct	16 Feb - 20 Oct
Sika	M	1 May - 31 July	21 Oct - 30 June
	F	1 Mar - 31 Oct	16 Feb - 20 Oct
Roe	M	1 Nov - 31 Mar	21 Oct - 31 Mar
	F	1 Mar - 31 Oct	1 Apr - 20 Oct
Red/Sika Hybrids	M	No closed season (Under review)	21 Oct - 30 June
	F	No closed season (Under review)	16 Feb - 20 Oct

There is no statutory close season for muntjac or Chinese Water Deer. It is recommended that when culling female muntjac, immature or heavily pregnant does should be selected to avoid the risk of leaving dependant fawns.

SAFETY

Always ensure that there is a solid backstop behind the deer before taking the shot and that you have an uninterrupted view of the background.

Never assume that thicket woodland will stop a bullet, or, that a thicket is unoccupied.

Always check that the line of shot is unobstructed.

Shooting from high seats (in woodland) is generally safer than shooting from ground level but rifles must always be unloaded before climbing in and out of a high seat.

Always check the bore of your rifle before loading especially if there is the slightest danger of the bore having been fouled with mud or snow.

Always apply the safety catch after loading and do not release it until about to take the shot.

Always unload your rifle before entering a house or vehicle.

Always remove the round from the breech before crossing an obstacle.

If, for any reason, it is necessary to leave a rifle in a (locked) vehicle, ensure that it is out of sight and remove the bolt and ammunition where practicable carry them with you.

TAKING A SHOT

Safety is paramount - never take a shot if there is the slightest doubt about safety.

Always identify your deer and ensure that no other deer, or any other animal are behind it which may be wounded by your shot passing through the target.

Never fire at a deer unless you are absolutely sure that it is well within your effective killing range.

Always ensure that, except at very close ranges, your deer is broadside on. Never take a head shot as this often results in a shattered jaw or nose-bone.

A broadside shot through heart or lungs is strongly recommended.

Never take a shot at a running deer - sooner or later this will result in a wounded deer (the exception being a second shot at a wounded deer). If in any doubt over any shot don't fire.

Before the shot, mark the position of the deer by some adjacent feature - bush, tree or rock, for example, and then, if the deer runs off into cover, always assume that you have hit it.

Immediately feed another round into the breech and then wait. You should learn to recognise the behaviour of deer, shot in different parts of the body, as this will dictate how long you should wait before following up. Whatever the circumstances, wait at least five minutes.

You should then approach the spot where the deer was standing and search for signs such as hair and blood. If you cannot find the carcase, do not give up. Follow the blood trail slowly, if possible with the aid of a trained dog. At all times be prepared to shoot again if necessary, but remember that at a range of a few metres the bullet will strike below the point of aim.

CARCASE HANDLING

All responsible stalkers must be capable of gralloching and inspecting a deer carcase. It is advisable to take lessons from a professional, or an appropriate training course.

Carcasses should be gralloched immediately after shooting and the pluck cleaned out as soon as possible - within 30 minutes in the summer.

After gralloching, the carcase should be hung up to drain, and as soon as possible, transferred to a cool, dry, fly-proof store with good ventilation.

Even in very cold weather, carcasses left to lie overnight may be spoiled and may be attacked by predators in any weather.

Produced jointly by The British Association for Shooting and Conservation and The British Deer Society.

The British Association
for Shooting & Conservation
Marford Mill
Rossett
Wrexham LL12 0HL
Tel: 01244 573 000
www.basc.org.uk

The British Deer Society
Fordingbridge
Hants
SP6 1EF
Tel: 01425 655 434
www.bds.org.uk

This code is endorsed by:

Deer Commission for Scotland
Knowsley
82 Fairfield Road
Inverness
IV3 5LH
Tel: 01463 231 751
www.dcs.gov.uk

The Deer Initiative
P.O. Box 2196
Wrexham
LL14 6YH
Tel: 0870 774 3677
Tel: 01463 231 751
www.thedeerinitiative.org.uk

APPENDIX 4

THE BRITISH DEER SOCIETY

The British Deer Society is a registered charity devoted to the welfare of the six species of deer found wild within the UK. The Society does the following:

Provides expert information to both members and non-members alike on all matters relating to deer and their management

Promotes, funds and collates research into subjects which may extend our knowledge of deer and their habits and result in their more humane treatment

Provides information and advice to various statutory agencies and other institutions on a wide range of subjects, including the impact of deer on the countryside, their integration with other land management interests, the prevention of road traffic accidents and the promotion of a valuable natural resource

Works with government bodies to ensure regulation is practical and sensible, and has the welfare of deer as one of its primary objectives

Publishes an internationally recognised, quarterly Journal covering a broad spectrum of deer related topics

Operates an active website: www.bds.org.uk with a range of information on deer species, research and deer interest topics such as branch news plus printable posters and educational leaflets – the website hosts an on-line shop run through the trading arm of the society which supplies a multitude of products – books, videos, CD's, and deer related items

Offers a varied programme of training courses in the UK to improve the skills necessary for the humane management of wild deer; including a web based distance learning programme for DSC Level 1 accessed through the website

BDS Training

All courses are delivered by specialist instructors providing courses for all levels of experience, they can also tailor training to specific needs.

Deer Stalking Certificate Level 1 Training Course
Distance Learning towards Deer Stalking Certificate Level 1
Deer Stalking Certificate Level 2 Awareness Training
BDS Deer Management Course
BDS Range Conducting Officers Course
Ammunition Re-loading Course

For details please contact:

The British Deer Society, Burgate Manor, Fordingbridge, SP6 1EF
Tel: 01425 655434
E-Mail: education@bds.org.uk
education@bds.org.uk
Website: www.bds.org.uk

BDS Membership

Subscribing members with a complete range of deer interests

Deer watchers, photographers and artists, conservationists, deer managers and stalkers, professionals, scientists, and researchers

Regional branches throughout the UK and links throughout the world

Local activities and events both social and educational with talks, demonstrations, field and range days

For details please contact:
The British Deer Society, Burgate Manor, Fordingbridge, SP6 1EF

Telephone: 01425 655434
Fax: 01425 655433
E-Mail: admin@bds.org.uk

INDEX

Accessories 6, 93
Aggression 18, 39, 46, 65, 186
Alarm posture 31
Albinism 34
Ammunition 6, 76, 78, 85, 94, 96, 99, 100, 108, 109, 200, 207, 209, 211
Anthrax 173
Antler cycle 36
Antler malformation 178
Antlers 5, 16, 27, 28, 35, 36, 37, 40, 45, 54, 56, 68, 162, 163, 178, 179, 188
Artificial feeding 54
Asia 15
Asian range 17

Backstop 123, 126, 131, 134, 135, 139, 144, 209
Ballistic tables 108
Bambi factor 56
barking 18, 48, 50, 121, 130
Barking Deer 18
Basic Stalker Training 5, 69
Bent-nosed syndrome 180
Binoculars 6, 83, 87, 88, 89, 92, 96, 105, 115, 120, 122, 141, 145, 208
Bipods 87
Black muntjac 17
Bleeding 146
Blood trail 140, 141, 142, 143, 193, 209

Bluebells 25, 26, 42, 186
Bore Sighting 6, 101, 111
Bounty 185
Bovine tuberculosis 173
Breeding Cycle 5, 45, 192
British Deer Society 4, 7, 13, 66, 70, 166, 192, 197, 198, 199, 200, 201, 206, 210, 211, 212
Broken canines 178
Browse line 42, 53, 64
Buck fever 135
Built up areas 56, 61, 62, 74
Bullet design 100
Butchery 7, 154, 190

Calibres 6, 71, 75, 76, 77, 100, 105, 108, 130, 193
Calling 4, 6, 128, 129, 130, 131, 132, 134
Camouflage 6, 59, 90, 91, 92, 113, 126, 131
Campylognathie 180
Canine tusks 16, 37, 40, 178, 179
Carcase contamination 146
Census Techniques 5, 62
Chiller cabinets 151
Chinese muntjac 5, 16, 17, 29
Chinese Water deer 16, 27, 28, 29, 71, 183, 199, 208
Clothing 6, 90, 91, 94, 114, 131, 200
Collimator 101, 111

Commercial Potential 7, 187
Commercialism 188
Communication 5, 47, 130
Compulsory Deer Manager Training 7, 190
Concealment 6, 113
Conseil International de la Chasse 166
Contraceptive drugs 56
Corbett, Jim 121
Coursing 72, 184
Crops 25, 42, 55, 116, 117, 118, 206, 207
Cull 5, 11, 12, 47, 55, 64, 65, 66, 68, 69, 119, 188

DEFRA 174, 177
Deterrents 5, 56, 58, 197
Dicrocerus 15
Digestive systems 41, 42, 185
Diseases 7, 170, 171, 173, 174, 181, 182, 198
Distribution 16, 21
Dogs 6, 15, 20, 53, 54, 55, 72, 133, 141, 142, 143, 173, 198
Dressed weight 30
Drink 43
Driven counts 63
Droppings 52, 53, 174
DSC1 6, 69, 70, 77, 81, 192, 199, 201
DSC2 70, 199
Duke of Bedford 18
Dung count 63

213

Ear defenders 86, 102
Electric fences 57
Establishment 5, 20, 183
Euthanasia 73, 74
Exit pupil 88, 89
External parasites 7, 65, 169, 170, 171
Eye relief 99

Facial markings 32
Fallow 13, 16, 26, 27, 39, 76, 174, 185, 198, 200, 208
Fawn 30, 33, 45, 46, 47, 55, 66, 67, 131, 132, 135, 182, 194, 195
Fea's muntjac 16
Feeding 23, 25, 39, 41, 42, 43, 44, 45, 47, 52, 54, 57, 65, 68, 69, 116, 117, 118, 119, 120, 122, 123, 134, 171, 173, 182, 185, 186
Fencing 24, 56, 57, 58, 62, 198
Fighting 37, 40, 65, 178
Firearms Certificate 81, 86, 95
Firearms certificates 61, 191
Follow-Up 6, 95, 139, 201
Foodstuffs 5, 40, 43, 44, 56, 118, 185
Foot and mouth 174, 182
Footwear 91, 122
Forestry 20, 25, 181, 184, 197, 198, 199, 206
Fox 28, 47, 56, 61, 67, 71, 75, 78, 130, 173, 182, 195
France 19
Fraying 25, 37, 40, 44, 49, 50, 68, 181

Free-floating 111
Frontal glands 32, 48, 49

Game License 71
Game meat standards 193
Game shooting 23, 142, 182, 193
Gardens 22, 25, 41, 181, 182, 184, 197
General Appearance 5, 34
Gestation period 46
Giant muntjac 17
Gralloch 6, 13, 60, 67, 94, 95, 139, 145, 146, 150, 168, 169, 173
Graticule 83, 84, 98, 99, 101
Grooming 45
Growth Cycle 5, 35, 38, 58, 68

Habitat 5, 20, 21, 22, 25, 40, 41, 43, 63, 64, 87, 172, 183, 184, 187
Hats 91
Head shot 136, 137, 209
Health & Safety 124, 191
Hearing 86, 114, 121, 130, 143
High seats 6, 116, 117, 119, 123, 124, 126, 128, 133, 134, 209
Hummelism 179
Hybridisation 20

Immuno-contraception 184
Impact on Other Wildlife 7, 185
Indian muntjak 16, 17, 18, 19, 20
Injuries 54, 73, 178
Interaction 39, 45, 182, 185

Internal Parasites 7, 65, 172
Keds 7, 65, 169, 170
Knives 6, 92, 157

Law 70, 71, 74, 75, 78, 81, 107, 174, 185, 191, 192, 193, 194, 197, 207
Leaf muntjac 17
Legal liability 124
Legislation 7, 184, 185, 191, 192, 193, 207
Lens 82, 83, 84, 85, 88, 89, 110
Lice 7, 169, 170, 171
Life-span 53
Line of vision 115
Live capture 62, 72
Liver fluke 172
Low seats 126
Lung worms 172
Lyme Disease 171
Lymph nodes 7, 175, 176
Lymphatic system 174, 175

Magnification 82, 83, 88, 131
Major organs 135
Malnutrition 56
Mating 46
Melanism 34
Miocene 15
Mobile telephones 133
Mounts 82, 84, 98, 99
Muntjac venison 189, 190, 202
Muzzle blast 80

Neck shot 108, 136
Night shooting 194

Oestrus 39, 45, 48, 66, 130

Paint and pins 140
Parallel walking 40
Pedicles 16, 18, 28, 32, 35, 40, 68, 162, 179
Pelage 5, 30
Permanent seats 125
Plaque 164
Pluck 175, 210
Polydactylism 178
Point of aim 103, 104, 105, 106, 108, 136, 137, 208, 210
Point of impact 105
Portable high seat 116, 117, 124, 125
Predation 47, 182, 183
Protection 25, 40, 71, 86, 110, 112, 197, 198, 206

Reaction to Shot 6, 137
Red deer 77, 85, 114, 179, 187
Reeves muntjac 16
Reloading 78, 100
Repellents 58
Rib Faced Deer 18
Ricochet 134
Rifle maintenance 6, 109
Right to Roam 59, 194
Rigor mortis 153
Rinderpest 173
Road traffic accidents 26, 55, 58, 61, 64, 73, 178, 182, 184, 191, 198, 211
Roe 11, 12, 13, 16, 24, 25, 27, 28, 39, 48, 50, 51, 53, 64, 68, 71, 78, 94, 96, 106, 108, 119, 120, 128, 129, 130, 143, 154, 173, 174, 179, 185, 186, 187, 189, 193, 197, 198, 202, 208
Roe sack 94, 96

Roosevelt's muntjac 17
Rucksack 94, 96, 105, 109, 127, 177

Safety 6, 23, 56, 60, 61, 69, 70, 109, 111, 124, 125, 133, 134, 135, 144, 191, 193, 194, 209
Salt licks 118
Satellite populations 184
Scent 44, 46, 47, 48, 49, 73, 114, 123, 126, 127, 132, 133, 141, 142
Scent glands 47
Scrapes 49, 50
Seasonal Approach 6, 116
Seasonal behaviour 35
Sexual maturity 45, 47
Sharpening 93
Sheath 92, 93, 95, 96
Shooting boxes 125
Shooting Technique 6, 102
Shotguns 71, 194, 195
Side winds 108
Sika 13, 27, 39, 76, 77, 183, 185, 208
Silencer 84
Skinning 13, 92, 153, 154, 157, 168
Sling 86, 87, 94, 95, 106, 110, 151
Snow 53, 140, 209
Social Structure 5, 39
Sound moderator 62, 81, 84, 86, 193
Sound recordings 130, 199
Spencer Chapman, F. 130
Sport hunters 188
Sticks 6, 89, 90, 96, 106, 127, 131
Sub-orbital glands 32, 48, 160

Summer coat 30, 31, 45
Survival rates 47
Suspect Health 7, 176
Swim 45

Tail 13, 27, 28, 31, 32, 33, 34, 50, 155
Tapeworm 173
Taxidermy 7, 168
Teeth 5, 37, 38, 40, 44, 49, 56, 66, 69, 72, 161, 163, 164, 178
Telescopic Sights 6, 81, 82, 83, 88, 106
Territory 5, 37, 39, 40, 44, 46, 47, 49, 178
Ticks 7, 65, 91, 169, 170, 171
Tooth wear 38, 69, 169
Tracks 5, 50, 118, 122, 127, 128, 136, 183
Trails 5, 46, 48, 50, 51
Training dogs 141, 198
Translocation 72, 184
Trapped 56, 61, 62, 72, 111
Trapping 62, 72
Tree guards 58
Trophy Measurement 7, 166, 197, 201
Trophy Preparation 7, 159
Truong Son muntjac 17
Tufted deer 15

Vehicles 26, 74, 95, 123, 177, 207, 209
Velvet 35, 36, 37, 45, 46, 178, 179
Venison market 7, 185, 189, 190

Walkie-talkie radios 95, 133

Washing powders 91
Weather 20, 43, 44, 53, 54, 84, 89, 92, 116, 128, 151, 153, 210
Weights 29, 30, 64, 65, 76, 186
Whipsnade 4, 19, 200
Wild boar 28, 76
Wind 44, 56, 108, 114, 115, 123, 126, 131, 143
Winter coat 16, 30, 31, 170
Woburn 4, 18, 19, 200

Yellow muntjac 17

Zeroing 6, 101, 102, 104, 105, 108, 208